THE COMPLETE GUIDE TO DOG LAW

The
COMPLETE
GUIDE
to
DOG LAW

Deidre E. Gannon, Esq.

HOWELL BOOK HOUSE
New York

MAXWELL MACMILLAN CANADA
Toronto

MAXWELL MACMILLAN INTERNATIONAL
New York   Oxford   Singapore   Sydney

Howell Book House
Macmillan Publishing Company
866 Third Avenue
New York, NY 10022

Maxwell Macmillan Canada, Inc.
1200 Eglinton Avenue East
Suite 200
Don Mills, Ontario M3C 3N1

Macmillan Publishing Company is part of the Maxwell Communication Group of Companies.

Library of Congress Cataloging-in-Publication Data
Gannon, Deidre E.
     The complete guide to dog law/by Deidre E. Gannon.
         p.   cm.
     ISBN 0-87605-658-3
     1. Dogs—Law and legislation—United States.   I. Title.
KF390.5.D6G36   1994
346.7304′7—dc20
[347.30647]   93–40138
                                                               CIP

Macmillan books are available at special discounts for bulk purchases for sales promotions, premiums, fund-raising, or educational use. For details, contact:

Special Sales Director
Macmillan Publishing Company
866 Third Avenue
New York, NY 10022

Book design by Susan Hood

1   3   5   7   9   10   8   6   4   2

Printed in the United States of America

Dedication

This book is dedicated to a variety of people who gave me the support and encouragement necessary to make it through law school and beyond.

Especially supportive were Rick Tomita, Bill Scolnik, Annette Mellinger, Leslie Walden and Gabe Moyette. To Ch. Ganymede's Matador De Pampas and Ch. Ganymede's Stormy Weather, who somehow survived it all, my special appreciation. Last, but certainly not least, is my father, Edward L. O'Hara III, without whom the dream would have ended in midstream.

Acknowledgments

Many thanks to those attorneys who helped with research, sent copies of any and all interesting material they came across and generally supported the project.

Especially to Carlos Enrique Vergara, Leslie Slade and Susan Claypoole.

A special thank-you to my editor, Seymour Weiss, who will one day realize that being prompt in all other aspects of life does not necessarily apply to my writing.

Contents

Contents

Introduction

Like my Argentine Dogos, I am, at least temporarily, a rare breed. That is, I am one of a handful of attorneys throughout the United States who are willing to take on cases involving dogs and dog people.

To many this may seem a minor-league specialty in the larger scheme of our litigious society. However, to anyone faced with a dog-related problem, an experienced dog law attorney can provide welcome relief after a long and frustrating search.

Dog law is unique in that the legal experience is secondary to the dog background. The combination is the key. Furthermore, this is a relatively new area that places the attorney in the role of an educator to the courts. Without a thorough understanding of the foundation upon which a given conflict arose, it is difficult to fashion a mutually acceptable remedy. Of course, an adventurous spirit that welcomes challenges is a necessary prerequisite to both the participation in dog events and the practice of dog law.

In recent years, our private little world has come under direct and indirect attacks from seemingly every imaginable direction. The restrictions being placed on dog ownership and activities are increasing. The "pit bull" mania seems endless. At the same time animal rights activists have launched a national campaign to ban breeding. While the causes of our problems may be self-evident, the solution is going to be complex and require long-term dedication.

The basis upon which dog owner and non-owner alike can build a peaceful coexistence is knowledge and cooperation. However, during the transition we dog owners can no longer afford to bury our heads in the sand and assume our little world is safe from outside influences. Recent history has proved just how wrong we have been.

This book is my small contribution to the overall effort. The intent is to provide nuts-and-bolts information that will assist you in preventing problems before they occur or, at least, to minimize their impact.

While no book can make you a self-sufficient legal expert, this book can assist you in dealing with the essentials of day-to-day dog ownership as well as developing the ability to recognize when outside assistance is necessary.

Where possible, I have tried to avoid the legalese that complicates understanding. If a concept can only be expressed in legal terminology, I have tried to define it as simply and concisely as possible. However, do not confuse easy reading with simple solutions. There are none.

An understanding of dog terminology is, of course, assumed.

Disclaimer

This book is not intended to dispense legal advice. Only your attorney is capable of evaluating your specific situation and advising you how best to proceed. Neither the author nor the publisher takes any responsibility for your use of the information contained herein in order to act on your own behalf.

THE COMPLETE GUIDE TO DOG LAW

1

The American Legal System

THE basic law of the United States is the Common Law of England. This system, established by the original colonists, has been adopted by most of the fifty states. The notable exception is Louisiana, which, true to its early French influence, adopted the Napoleonic Code.

The common law system is influenced by various factors. This allows for the flexibility that is both to our benefit and to our detriment.

When the legislatures enact statutes they are not necessarily worded clearly or correctly. It is then up to the courts to interpret and apply these statutes to a given matter. These decisions are then recorded and organized for later reference. Some of these decisions may be important enough so that they, in turn, are codified—enacted as statutes or used to amend existing ones. Others may simply provide guidance as to how future cases may be decided. Further illumination may be obtained from the principles in each area that have been formulated and tested over time. The law may also be influenced by custom and usage as well as by societal value judgments (i.e., prohibition, anti-smoking legislation and proposed breeding bans).

1

While confusing, the system is beneficial in that there is a great deal of flexibility built in so that the law can grow and change as the people and their society evolve. However, the detriment lies in crowded court dockets, for, in many cases, there are no clear-cut answers. As our society has grown and become more complex, our laws have followed the same path to the point that we are probably one of the most litigious societies in the world.

Since we will be dealing primarily with federal, state and local law throughout this book, the following is a brief overview of each one's place within the whole scheme.

Federal law derives from the Constitution of the United States, which specifically reserves to Congress the right to make laws affecting interstate and foreign commerce, provide for the common defense, coin money, regulate immigration and deal with all matters relating to interstate and foreign relations.

In recent years, federal law has gained a new prominence because of the expansion of business across state lines. Today, almost everyone is engaged in some form of interstate commerce and subject to some form of federal regulation. This has become necessary in order to provide uniform treatment of like parties throughout the United States.

State law also derives from the United States Constitution in that legislative power not expressly delegated to the federal government is reserved to the states. Thus, most of the laws relating to the health and general welfare of a community and its citizens are passed by state legislatures within the limitations set by the federal and state constitutions.

However, the ability to pass local ordinances is dependent upon the enabling legislation present under the state constitution or that enacted by the state legislature. Like the states, localities are responsible for the health and welfare of their citizens on a smaller scale in individual cities and towns.

More recent additions to the hierarchy of laws and government are the condominium associations, which through recorded master deeds and bylaws are empowered to enact rules and regulations for the health and welfare of their individual owners. Townhome communities set up as home-owner associations operate on the same theory but usually have less latitude than condos.

Finally, one of the most important reasons to have an understanding of the pyramidal structure of government from the lowest to the highest is the concept of preemption. For example, when various New Jersey municipalities started passing breed-specific legislation, a number of counties started looking into county-wide ordinances. If passed, these county enactments would have preempted that area from the purview of the local government. In the case of New Jersey, a state non-breed-specific vicious dog law was enacted which preempted the area from the purview of all the local forms of government. The next step would be for the federal government to enact legislation in this area, preempting the area from all those below that level. This is usually done in cases where uniformity is desired throughout the governmental unit and the issue is important enough to attract the attention of the entity above the one currently acting in the pyramidal structure.

However, though preemption may seem to be the solution to many problems, it is not something any governmental unit takes lightly. For one governmental unit to take authority away from another, there must be a serious situation requiring uniformity throughout. Thus, federal legislation in the area of vicious dogs is still a goal to be achieved. Meanwhile, in every aspect of our lives we need to understand how government works and be able to deal effectively at all levels.

2

The Concept of Dogs as Property

PEOPLE have a wide variety of words with which to characterize their dogs—from the call name to any number of anthropomorphic terms. No one thinks of that living, breathing befurred friend as merely a "thing," yet that is how a dog is treated under the law. A dog is in essence property of the owner.

By definition, "property" refers to one's exclusive right to possess, use and dispose of a thing. This is the concept of ownership or title. Dogs have no individual rights, cannot own anything else individually and cannot inherit money or property. They are essentially the same as any other appliance.

While there have been changes in recent years due to several studies that have established the positive effects of dog ownership, there is not yet a generally accepted judicial treatment of dogs. Depending upon the state, there are three theories that predominate. The most often used concept is that of basic property. This category includes just about any inanimate, movable item one can own, including furniture, appliances or clothing. If damaged, the value will be determined by the difference between the original purchase price and the value of the property as damaged or the cost of repair. If destroyed, replacement cost is usually the determining factor of value. However, replacement cost of a dog is usually that of a puppy.

A much more reasonable approach is to treat a dog as "special" property. This allows for a variety of factors to be considered in the valuation process. These include time and money invested in bringing the dog from a puppy to an adult, breeding life, show career or other value-enhancing aspects. Thus, the dog is granted a status of its own. However, while considered better than a simple appliance, a dog is still considered much less than a person. The concept of property still applies.

A related treatment is that of "unique" property. This concept is most often used in real estate, but has occasionally been applied to dogs. A dog is unique in that no two dogs are absolutely alike. Thus a dog can be considered irreplaceable. However, this treatment would apply only in disputes where a particular dog is in question. As in real estate transactions, a purchaser could force an owner to deliver the specific dog contracted for rather than another one even if it is of equal quality.

Though progress has been made in how courts treat dogs, the particular elements that owners want taken into consideration when value is being determined are still vague concepts. While almost everyone understands that a large part of the value of a horse or cow lies in its ability to reproduce, the same cannot be said of dogs. Whether it is because of the dog's lower monetary value or the sheer number of dogs in our society has yet to be established. However, it is not helping matters that animal rights activists are seeking to curtail or completely eliminate the breeding of purebred dogs.

The same problems exist when conformation and obedience showing and training are taken into consideration by the courts. Judges and juries have no understanding of all of the work, time and money that is expended in titling dogs. While you and I know that an eight-week obedience course does not an OTCH make and a two-day handling clinic does not win you Best in Show at Westminster, those outside the fancy think of a dog as merely a domestic animal kept in the home.

The insularity of the dog world has created its own problems. There is a large amount of information people need to have in order to form sound judgments, many of which will go against preconceived notions of dog ownership. The requirement that all AKC-affiliated clubs have public education coordinators is a step in the right direction.

A concept allied to that of *ownership and title* is that of *possession and control*. A dog is not responsible for its actions. The owner or some other person having possession and control of the dog is the responsible party. The idea that possession is nine-tenths of the law still has validity. It is the action or non-action of the owner, not the dog, that is at issue.

This is the area where breed-specific legislation has tried to define the acceptable level of control under the concept of public safety. Prior to the "pit bull" scare, it was assumed that dog owners would take necessary precautions to protect their dogs and the public. If a person did not exert sufficient control over his dog and an incident occurred, the legal process would provide the remedy. For the most part, this system worked. However, once the media blew the whole situation out of proportion, the "pit bull" problem became a societal problem. Public outcry resulted in quickly drafted legislation. While well intentioned, most of this type of legislation was inaccurate, vague and only selectively enforceable.

From the dog owners' perspective, breed-specific legislation is a nightmare which has the potential to affect any breed and/or mixed breed that meets certain criteria.

At their worst, these laws authorize the taking of someone's property without compensation while imposing civil, and sometimes criminal, penalties on the owner. Often, these laws violate our due process rights in that the property can be destroyed without benefit of a hearing. At their best, the due process requirements are carefully protected but leave the dog at risk of destruction while the process is being carried out.

A much more detailed discussion of breed-specific legislation appears in Chapter 12, LEGISLATIVE ACTION.

Bailment

Another related property concept is *bailment*. Though this term is rarely used in dog situations, bailment is actually a frequent occurrence. Bailment means that a person other than the owner is in legal possession of the dog. The most common examples are boarding kennel operators and professional handlers and trainers.

A boarding kennel is in the business of housing and caring for dogs other than its own. The owner (bailor) places the dog in the possession of the kennel personnel (bailee) for a specific period of time, usually under an oral or written agreement. Thus the kennel is in legal possession of the dog and has accepted certain responsibilites for that property of another. Primary among these is the duty to return the dog to the owner in as good condition as it was received.

The same is true of professional handlers, who are in the business of handling dogs other than their own in competition. Whether the dog is legally placed in their possession for a short or longer period of time, the duty of maintaining the dog in at least the same condition as received still applies. Again, there is usually an oral or written agreement that outlines the terms and conditions of the bailment.

While boarding kennels and professional handlers are the most often seen forms of bailments, many other situations fall into this category. These include hospitalization at a veterinarian's office, dog-sitting in the home, dog-walking services, dog-sitting for friends or family, and grooming establishments where the dog is left while the services are being performed. This concept could also be extended to shelters in situations where the dog is impounded during legal proceedings and the dog is ultimately returned to the owner.

Conversion

Should the dog be injured or destroyed in any way during a bailment situation, the bailee (caretaker) is said to have converted the owner's property. Remember that the bailee has assumed the duty of delivering the dog back to the owner in as good condition as received. Again this is a valuation issue. An injury to the dog reduces its value. For example, you and your professional handler get into an argument and your prize bitch is returned to you after having been spayed. There is a vast difference in value between a bitch capable of reproduction and one that is not. Another example is when a pet-sitter does not securely latch the gate to a dog's kennel or yard, the dog gets out, runs into the street, gets hit by a car and dies. While the first example involves malicious conduct on the part of the handler and the second example is simply negligence, both are considered *conversions*.

In both these examples, conversion of the property results in a loss to the owner. If legal action is initiated, we are back to the valuation problems discussed earlier. In both cases, compensatory damages—those designed to compensate the owner for loss or reduction in property value—are involved. Whether or not punitive damages will be awarded for the malicious conduct on the part of the handler will be determined by the court. Punitive damages are meant to act as a deterrent against future acts of the same kind by the same person as well as a warning to others who might consider the same course of behavior.

Liens and Judgments

Further issues regarding title and possession concepts often arise in relation to monetary problems. Since dogs are property, technically a lien for unpaid bills could be placed against the owner's property interest in that dog. A lien is a claim against property that must be satisfied before clear title can be conveyed to another party. In some states, a handler's lien can be placed, the same as a mechanic's lien, without reducing the claim to judgment. In other states, a judgment must be in place and the lien is part of the execution on the judgment in that it provides the creditor with a secured interest in the property.

Another sticky situation arising from monetary conflicts is the continued possession of the dog by the person to whom money is owed. In most situations, the creditor was originally in legal possession of the dog. When the owner asks for the return of the property, the creditor demands that full payment be made first. If there is a valid dispute regarding the bill, the best approach is to petition the court for *replevin*, the return of the property to the owner. This will usually entail the posting of a bond equal to or greater than the debt claimed. The issues regarding the debt can be resolved in due course through the legal system.

As you can see, treating dogs as property creates an entirely different set of problems than expected when dealing with the legal system. This is where many people experience culture shock, because their dogs are often part of the family and they expect everyone to have the same approach and understanding. The chilling effect of a legal dispute regarding our dogs can come as quite a surprise and leave us grasping at straws. This is where competent legal counsel with dog experience can make a difference. If that is not available, then our ability to explain the situation clearly and succinctly can affect the outcome.

The emotional elements that often pervade dog-based conflicts must be put in their proper perspective if not eliminated altogether. Not everyone shares our passion and commitment to dogs and thereby hangs many an opening for grief.

3

The Dog in Modern Society

FOLLOWING a two-day hearing, a New Jersey judge ordered the renewal of an existing kennel license in an area zoned residential/agricultural and stated, "I have never seen a farm without a dog."

However, he further ruled that the license was non-transferable and would terminate upon the sale of the property involved. Little did we know at the time that this was only the beginning of a continuous battle to keep our dogs.

Early in this nation's history there is documentation of domesticated dogs living and/or working with people. The American Indians kept dogs in their camps and used them to haul their belongings from one location to another. Many were used in hunting. The early settlers brought dogs with them. Some breeds, such as the Louisiana Catahoula Leopard Dog, were native to this country. Others, such as Coonhounds, were developed here to meet various needs.

In areas that became densely populated, companion dogs and those noted for personal/property protection became popular. The police and military have used dogs, in war and peace, for various purposes. Service dogs, such as guide dogs, have a long history of valuable contributions to man's quality of life. Many studies have proven that dog ownership has beneficial physiological and psychological effects.

So where did it all go wrong? What happened to make the dog one of the most feared animals in our society today?

When asked these questions, most people would point to the media and the "pit bull" sensationalism. However, the trend toward placing restrictions on dog ownership was already in place when the "pit bull" incidents hit the press.

Whenever a situation threatens public health and safety, government at some level will intervene. One early example is dog licensing. This was enacted with the goal of ensuring that all dogs had current rabies vaccinations. As a nation with international borders, we cannot completely eradicate the problem, which flourishes in wildlife, but some form of control can lessen the potential for harm. An island community, such as Hawaii, which can totally eradicate rabies, will take this one step further in requiring an extended quarantine to make sure no infection is brought into the area.

If a culprit has to be selected as the main impetus toward animal control, it is most likely the industrial revolution, which created denser population centers. More people in a given area create more problems as well as the potential for conflict. There is a greater possibility of real or perceived situations erupting in nasty neighbor disputes when residences are mere yards apart than on farms that are miles apart.

In most cases there are more regulation and ownership restrictions on the East Coast, particularly in the Northeast, and the West Coast, specifically in areas of California. It is little wonder that so many dog people are moving to the South and Midwest.

The ordinances that are enacted most often include leash laws, scoop and/or curbing requirements, limits on the numbers of dogs per residence and mandatory licensing. Dogs may be banned from local parks and wildlife areas under a variety of theories. Densely populated communities, such as apartment complexes and condominiums, may ban dog ownership altogether. Some quasi-agricultural areas have been known to place a cap on the number of active kennel licenses that may exist in a given community. Unfortunately, since most areas do not differentiate between hobby and commercial kennels, this severely restricts the small private breeder who has a dog or two over the local limit.

Where breed-specific legislation exists, further restrictions are imposed. These include muzzling of the targeted breeds, specific kenneling designations and minimal insurance limits that are hard to obtain. These provisions will apply to dogs of that breed that already exist in the community. Usually there will be a cutoff date after which no new specimens of that breed will be allowed within the community (e.g., Dade County, Florida, and Denver, Colorado).

This is why it is very important to do your homework thoroughly before you decide to move into a community. Start with the local clerk and ask for all ordinances regarding dogs, cats and domestic pets. If you ask only for those concerning dogs, you may miss something enacted separately under a different designation (e.g., domestic pets) that just might impact upon you and your dogs at a later date. Remember that these ordinances are a matter of public record and ignorance of their existence and/or content is no defense when the municipality decides to take you to task for some inadvertent infraction.

In addition, you should visit the health and zoning officers. The health officer can confirm the ordinances provided by the local clerk and inform you of any additional requirements. If you are considering a kennel license in the area, usually the health officer is the first contact, followed by the zoning officer, especially if a variance is required. The clerk will get involved as the issuing authority for individual or kennel licenses.

Finally, check whether there are any pending ordinances that have to do with dogs, cats and/or domestic pets. Ask for copies before you sign the purchase contract, as these ordinances may make the difference in your choosing between

15

this community and the one next door. Also, inquire if they have had any problems with dogs in the area. A statement by the local clerk that they have major problems with stray dogs may very well indicate that a restrictive ordinance is just a matter of time.

Another good practice, once you move in, is to introduce yourself and one or more dogs to the local animal control office and police personnel. If your breed is not well known, provide information about temperament and behavior. Explain your interests and activities (i.e., show, obedience, search and rescue) in a positive and enthusiastic manner.

While this may seem like a lot of trouble, it will pay off in the event there is an incident with your dog. Even an accidental escape from the property can result in panic and hot tempers when certain breeds or perceptions of a certain breed are involved. Remember, to the uninitiated, a Boxer, a Chinese Shar-Pei or even a Pug could raise the cry of "Oh my God, it's a pit bull!"

Assuming all has gone well and you are now safely ensconced in a friendly, tolerant community with your dogs settled and happy, you would think that you could relax and proceed with your life. Not so. You must always be alert to developing situations, pending ordinances and changing trends within the community. Any of these can pose a problem for you and your dogs. The point is not to be surprised. It is much harder to fight public outcry and pending ordinances than it is to resolve the problem as it is occurring.

Case law in this area is divided. Some courts agree that a lawful use that has become a nuisance because the community has changed can be made to shut down or move. However, the person who is forced to leave is entitled to some compensation. Other courts adhere to the "coming to the nuisance" theory, according to which a residential landowner will be denied relief if he knowingly moved into a neighborhood where a given activity is already in existence. He cannot call upon the legal system to make the location of his residence suitable when it was not so when he selected it originally.

Make sure you know what constitutes a nuisance in your community. Meticulously adhere to all health regulations applicable to kennels whether or not you have or intend to apply for a kennel license. In other words, establish your defense before the complaint is filed.

Try your best to establish and maintain amicable relationships with your neighbors. If nothing else, keep the lines of communication open so that they feel comfortable coming to you with a problem rather than running to the local authorities. However, should a situation arise that results in legal action, defend yourself and your dogs.

4

Dog People:
Liability Considerations

LIABILITY refers to responsibility for one's conduct, which includes any action or failure to act.

In most cases where a person is held liable for an injury there must be a duty owed to the person who is injured and the person responsible must have breached that duty. Only in strict liability can there be liability without fault. This usually pertains to an activity that has an inherent risk of injury, such as handling explosives or harboring wild animals. Holding a person liable without a showing of negligence tends to discourage dangerous activities while not totally prohibiting any social benefit they may have.

There have been attempts to impose strict liability on dog owners in certain states, specifically New Jersey. Breed-specific legislation often imposes this standard on the breeds listed in the statute.

The standard of proof required in civil cases, other than strict liability situations, is a preponderance of the evidence, when one side's evidence is more convincing to the trier of fact than the opposing evidence. It refers to proof that leads the trier of fact to find that the existence of the fact at issue is more probable than not. In an exceptional civil case the standard may be raised to the clear-and-convincing stage, which is more than a preponderance standard but less than the beyond-a-reasonable-doubt standard imposed in criminal cases. However, in strict liability situations all one must show is that the event occurred and the injuries were proximately caused by the defendant's activity. No showing of negligence under any standard is required.

As there is a potential for liability in just about anything we do, it is not surprising that dog people are becoming more aware of their vulnerability.

Most situations will be covered under tort law. A *tort* is a private or civil wrong or injury resulting from a breach of a legal duty that exists by virtue of society's expectations regarding interpersonal conduct, rather than by contract or other private relationship. The essential elements of a tort are the existence of a legal duty owed by a defendant to a plaintiff, a breach of that duty and the resulting damage to the plaintiff.

Since dogs are property and therefore have no legal rights of their own, the duty is owed to or by the owner of that dog, depending upon the situation.

A dog owner owes the general public a duty of reasonable care in confining/controlling his dog so that it does not bite or otherwise injure people or their property. A duty of reasonable care is that degree of care which, under the circumstances, would be ordinarily or usually exercised by, or might be reasonably expected from, an ordinarily prudent person. This is the *reasonable man standard*. A reasonable man is a hypothetical person who "exercises those qualities of attention, knowledge and judgment which society requires of its members for the protection of their own interests and the interests of others" (Restatement Torts 2d, 283(b)).

On the other hand, trainers and handlers would be required to adhere to a higher standard of care because of their specialized training and experience. Thus they will be held to the standard of the reasonable trainer or handler. In this case, establishing a breach of the duty is more difficult because neither is licensed by a national or local agency. While a few organizations do provide some sort of recognition to these professionals, this is a voluntary procedure and many are not members. It is a little too easy to declare yourself a handler or a trainer without meeting any professional criteria. The same is true of groomers in most states. Usually, a groomer is required to be licensed only if he uses regulated chemicals (e.g., dips).

Unlike handlers, trainers and groomers, veterinarians have to meet certain criteria and satisfy certain minimal testing and educational requirements in order to be licensed. While they still have to meet a higher standard of care, that of a reasonable veterinarian, there is a licensing agency with the ability to discipline its members.

Boarding kennels are in an in-between situation. They are required to have a kennel license as mandated by the municipality and also must satisfy the health department requirements for their state. They are subject to inspection as well. Operators will also be required to meet the standard of a reasonable boarding kennel operator. On the other hand, the hobby kennel is often not subject to licensing and inspection requirements. There is some diversity in boarding kennels, but much more among hobby kennels. While a higher standard may be imposed, proof of a breach of that heightened duty may be more difficult to obtain even in a given area. Luckily most transactions involving kennels will be contractual relationships and the breach, if any, will be a breach of contract.

Dog club liability at a show is apparent, but insurance is generally required by the owners of the show site. A heightened standard of care would be imposed since this is a specialized activity and the club members are presumed to have experience in the conduct of shows. This would apply to show superintendents to an even greater degree.

Dog Club Incorporation

Many clubs mistakenly believe that the mere act of incorporation protects the directors and officers from personal liability. This is not necessarily true, because the protection afforded by a corporate charter depends on how the business is conducted on a continuous basis. When a dispute arises involving a corporation, the first thing an attorney will look for is a way to "pierce the corporate veil." Piercing the corporate veil is the process of imposing liability for corporate activity, in disregard of the corporate form, on a person or entity other than the offending corporation itself. Generally, the corporate form isolates both individuals and parent organizations from liability for corporate misdeeds. However, the courts will ignore the corporate entity and strip the officers and directors of the limited liability that they usually enjoy when the incorporation itself and/or the continued conduct of corporate affairs fails to measure up to the legal expectations and requirements of that corporate form—for-profit or not-for-profit entities.

Before incorporating a dog club it is wise to seek legal counsel. If you do not, then in order to avoid the common pitfalls, you should familiarize yourself with the statutory scheme for the form of corporation you wish to set up, as well as the case law on the existence of the corporation and how others have had the corporate veil pierced. Also, always remember that a dog club is a business and must function as one within the statutory scheme and the governing documents.

Governing documents of a corporation include the articles of incorporation, which are very generalized in their language in order to give the corporate entity the flexibility to operate in a broad range of activities. The constitution and bylaws make up the primary framework in which that corporation functions. They must be adhered to to the letter or be amended when a problem arises.

The American Kennel Club has a sample set of constitution and bylaws applicable to several kinds of clubs. Overall these are composed well and allow enough flexibility in which to operate. While a forming club is expected to draft and adopt the sample constitution and bylaws, minor changes may be acceptable for good reasons. However, personally, I consider some areas to be too broad and giving the officers and directors of the club too much power, specifically in the discipline department. While there are due process requirements in place through a hearing board as well as an appeal process in certain circumstances, specifically expulsion, to the entire membership the question remains as to what actually constitutes conduct detrimental to the breed or the club. While I am sure a number of actions come to mind, consider that almost anything someone doesn't approve of could become the basis for disciplinary charges being filed. Finally, the matter can ultimately be taken to a court of law as a civil suit against the club. That, however, is expensive and time-consuming.

Service Dog Organizations

Everyone is familiar with the signs exempting guide dogs from whatever constraints have been imposed on access to public buildings. However, a new group of assistance programs has developed in the last decade. These service dogs are beneficial to man in very specialized areas. In assisting their human partners they should be accorded the same rights as guide dogs for the blind. This has not necessarily always been the case.

Many states have, in recent years, adopted statutory schemes to accord rights of access to service dogs, service dog trainees, owners and trainers. However, while the law gives them the right of access, many organizations, especially schools, have fought them, saying that the presence of the service dog is unnecessary because the school can provide the same or better services required by the student and that the presence of the dog is disruptive. Though a few administrative hearings have been held over the last few years, the result has usually been that the student and the parents end up transferring the student to a more "dog-friendly" school.

This is a new area and it will be interesting to monitor the progress that continues to be made by the service dog organizations. It is hoped that one day service dogs will be accepted with the equanimity that is enjoyed by guide dogs for the blind. Someday the exemption signs will read "service dogs" rather than just "guide dogs."

5

Anatomy of a Contract I: Writing the Sales Agreement

BUYING and selling dogs are business transactions, pure and simple. One party offers to sell, the other party offers to buy, and the two come to an agreement as to the price and terms of the transaction. While there may be some negotiation during the agreement process, there is nothing particularly difficult about an outright sale.

Once an agreement regarding the price and terms of the transaction is reached, the next logical step is to reduce it to written form. Yet nine out of ten people who end up in a dispute over a dog do not have a written contract. (Note that "contract" and "agreement" are used interchangeably to mean the same thing.)

The most frequent reason given for the lack of a written agreement is "I trusted him" or "I didn't want her to feel that I didn't trust her." In today's society, this reason is ridiculous. Buy and sell transactions are not a matter of trust; the handshake exchange is effectively a matter of historical curiosity; they are straightforward business transactions.

Dogs cost money, often sizable amounts. Any other purchase of the same financial magnitude would be governed by a contract. Yet dogs are bought and sold daily without benefit

25

of such a safeguard. If the investment is the same, why should the method be different? It shouldn't.

It is more likely that written agreements are few and far between because dog people are in the unenviable position of drafting their own contracts. There is no forms book or other resource guide with a canned Puppy/Dog Sales Agreement to fit each person's situation. In addition, there are few attorneys with sufficient dog knowledge to draft them on an individual or group basis. There are too many important considerations in dog transactions that the non-dog person simply does not know or understand. Also, attorney-drafted agreements are expensive.

Therefore, I have taken a nuts-and-bolts approach to the issue of contracts. I deal with the areas I take into consideration when drafting agreements. You may have others, as you should. No two breeds are exactly alike. No two transactions are exactly alike. And as with dogs, there are no perfect contracts. They are only as good as the drafter, through time and effort, can make them.

Contract drafting is both an art and a science.

In its essence, a sales contract is an agreement between two or more parties for the exchange of a good for money. While the exchange can be for an item or promise other than money, here, for simplicity's sake, we will make the assumption of an outright purchase involving money. Later chapters will deal with breeder's term, puppy-back stud fee contracts and other essential components.

While the ideal contract is one negotiated between the parties, this does not occur in most cases. Usually it is up to the one selling the puppy to have a contract prepared and ready to be signed before or at the time of delivery. The person selling the puppy, usually a breeder, is assumed to have greater knowledge as to what constitutes a proper agreement for the exchange. As most purchasers are looking for companion animals, this is probably true to some extent. However, knowledge as a breeder does not necessarily guarantee knowledgeable contract drafting.

By putting the obligation of contract drafting on the breeder, the purchaser creates a situation wherein he relies on the breeder for his dog knowledge but in the event of a dispute in which a clause is determined to be vague and must be interpreted by the court, the legal process will construe the clause against the drafter/breeder because he is the one presumed to have the greater knowledge. However, even in this situation, it is better to have one clause construed against you than the whole transaction questioned and redefined because no written contract exists at all. Consider it a learning process, for you won't make that mistake again.

Another reason for reducing an agreement to written form is the Statue of Frauds, which requires contracts to be in writing when the sales price exceeds $500 or when the agreement will not be completely performed within one year. The other requirements under this statute do not affect dog-related transactions and have been omitted here.

So now that you understand that you need a written agreement, the next step is to determine what you want to include in the contract.

The Thought Process

Before attempting to draft your sales agreement, you have to decide what you feel is very important and must be included, what is important and should be included, and what is somewhat important and may be included or negotiated between the parties. Once that list has been compiled, look closely at the language you are planning to use (i.e., "pet"/"breeding"/"show quality"). While you may understand what you mean by these terms, not everyone else does. Even fellow dog fanciers will vary in their understanding of what these terms mean. Therefore, it is important that you develop specific definitions so that the layman purchaser will understand what you mean by a particular word or phrase.

Next, examine the guarantees/warranties you wish to offer

the purchaser (e.g., hip dysplasia). Should this condition occur, how does the purchaser activate the clause? Will you require veterinarian certification, copies of X-rays or OFA readings when the dog reaches a particular age? What will you offer to do in the event this condition occurs? Replace the puppy, refund all or part of the purchase price or make another adjustment? Review each possible situation and assume it will happen. Detail what you see as your responsibilities and those of the purchaser. Be specific!

Next list all the terms that are negotiable or differ from contract to contract. These will contain provisions that will not vary and some that will. They will be handled by leaving spaces to be filled in as each contract is agreed upon between you and the purchaser. It is easier, and better business in the long run, to have one basic contract for every transaction. In order to make it flexible enough for variation, certain sections will be filled in on a case-by-case basis, whereas others can be deleted in their entirety and replaced with an addendum. If you redraft a contract for every sale, you run the risk of creating confusion and, perhaps, missing the inclusion of a term you consider very important.

Finally, review your lists, definitions and criteria for thoroughness and accuracy. This does not mean that they cannot be changed now or in the future. Rather, this is the basis from which you will begin to build your contract, one specifically tailored to your kennel and/or breeding program.

The Drafting Process

PARTIES

Name(s), addresses, other appropriate identification (i.e., identifying which party is the seller and which is the buyer).

SALES CONTRACT

This agreement, made this _____ day of _____,
199 ___, is between _____
(Seller) located at _____,
_____ _____ _____ and _____
(Buyer) residing at _____,
_____ _____ _____. Seller and Buyer
are collectively referred to as the "parties."

Note: If you regularly use your kennel name in transacting business the section denoting Seller would contain your name followed by "doing business as" _____
("DBA" may be substituted for the phrase "doing business as"). If either party is a corporation, state this as well as the state where incorporated.

DESCRIPTION OF PUPPY/DOG BEING SOLD

The Buyer agrees to purchase from the Seller a male/female puppy of the _____ breed from the
_____ (sire) X _____
(dam) litter whelped _____, 199___.
    The puppy shall be of _____ quality as determined by the breeder.

1. SHOW QUALITY is defined as a pick puppy that has the potential to be shown and titled in the conformation ring. Said puppy will be free of disqualifying faults at maturity as determined by the breed standard. Maturity is the period from 6 months of age until the dog becomes a Champion of record or two (2) years of age, whichever comes first.

2. BREEDING QUALITY is defined as a puppy that has the potential to develop into a dog of sufficient merit so that, while it may not title, it will have no genetic fault that would preclude breeding to a like or better dog.

3. PET QUALITY is defined as a puppy that has a disqualifying fault or other shortcoming that precludes showing and/or breeding. Said fault will not prevent the puppy from living an otherwise normal and healthy life.

PURCHASE PRICE

The purchase price of the puppy will be $_____ less the deposit of $_____. The balance is due on or before delivery of the puppy. Shipping charges are additional.

Note: Form of payment may also be specified (e.g., cash, money order, etc.). This is the paragraph that can be deleted in conditional sale contracts and replaced by an addendum detailing the terms.

GENERAL TERMS

Health, special conditions and paperwork.

The Seller certifies that, upon delivery, the puppy is in good health and has been immunized and wormed according to the attached health record. It is recommended that the puppy be taken to the buyer's veterinarian within 48 hours of receipt.

Note: The health record is incorporated by reference within the body of the contract.

Ears will be cropped prior to delivery. However, removal of stitches and post-cropping care are the responsibility of the buyer.

American Kennel Club registration will be provided within thirty (30) days of delivery. Puppies classified as pet quality will receive limited registration and must be spayed or neutered by one (1) year of age.

WARRANTIES

Warranties are assurances by the seller to the buyer of the existence of a fact upon which the buyer may rely without ascertaining that fact for himself. It amounts to a promise that the seller will indemnify the buyer for any loss if the fact warranted proves untrue. Warranties are made either overtly as in express warranties or by implication as in implied warranties.

Express warranties are contained within the written agreement. Implied warranties are incorporated by law. The implied warranty of merchantability and that of fitness for a particular purpose are the most common.

With the warranty of merchantability the seller attests that the dog is reasonably fit for the general purposes for which it has been sold—pet, breeding, show. The warranty of fitness for a particular purpose deems the dog suitable for the special purpose of the buyer (e.g., search and rescue, Schutzhund, drug detection, etc.), which will not be satisfied by mere fitness for general purposes.

The warranty of merchantability is relatively easy to comply with, as a dog is primarily a companion animal. Most puppies would be considered fit for the general purpose of a companion. The warranty of fitness for a particular purpose has more perils. If, during the discussion regarding the sale of the dog, the buyer states that he wants "to do Schutzhund," this could be considered a special purpose. If you respond that the dog should be able to do that, it could be construed that you had warranted the dog for that purpose. It is best to protect yourself by including the following in your agreements:

This dog is warranted only for the purpose of being a companion animal. While it may be capable of performing other functions, no warranty is given as to its fitness for any special purpose.

Express warranties are whatever you are willing to offer the buyer. However, keep in mind that those who often run afoul of lemon laws are those who either omit warranties or are not specific enough in their warranties against conditions like hip dysplasia or other genetic problems in a particular breed.

The following examples are warranties against hip dysplasia, deafness and general genetic problems:

The Seller guarantees the following:

a. The dog will be free from hip dysplasia of a genetic origin at the age of two (2) years as determined by the Orthopedic Foundation for Animals (OFA).
b. Show and breeding quality dogs will be able to hear in both ears. Pet quality dogs may be unilaterally deaf, but will not be bilaterally deaf. BAER (Brainstem Auditory Evoked Response) test results will be provided for each puppy.
c. The dog will be free from genetic problems that would preclude it from living an otherwise normal and healthy life.

Should the dog develop one or more problems enumerated above, the buyer shall have the option to:

a. Neuter the current dog and accept a replacement puppy of the same quality originally purchased. The replacement will be selected by the breeder from the next available litter and provided upon proof of neutering.
b. Neuter the dog and receive a partial refund of the purchase price. The refund will be the difference between the actual purchase price and that of a pet quality puppy from the same litter.

The seller reserves the right to have a second veterinarian of his/her choice evaluate the dog's condition before the guarantee will be honored, except in the case of OFA-evaluated hip X-rays.

RETURN POLICY

In the event the buyer is unable to keep the dog for any reason, he/she agrees to immediately contact the seller, who has the first option to accept the return of the dog. In the event of a resale, the original buyer must notify the seller and provide the new owner's name, address and phone number.

CONTRACT AMENDMENT

Any changes or additional terms to this Agreement must be in the form of an Addendum and signed by all parties.

SEVERABILITY

As stated previously, a contract is only as good as the drafter and we can all make mistakes. Thus, the following clause will maintain the integrity of the document should any clauses be declared invalid.

If any provision of the Agreement is or becomes void or unenforceable by force or operation of law, the other provisions shall remain valid and enforceable.

INTEGRATION CLAUSE

This is a very important paragraph that most dog people fail to include in their agreements. Essentially, it says that the entire agreement is contained within the four corners of the contract. This prevents any evidence of prior or contemporaneous understandings of the parties, either written or oral, from being presented in order to vary or contradict the contract.

The entire Agreement between the parties is contained herein.

LAW TO APPLY

Since one of the primary purposes of a contract is to prevent misunderstandings and keep you out of court, it is hoped that few, if any, disputes arise. However, if a dispute does occur, you certainly don't want to have to defend yourself on the other side of the country. This can happen. Pennsylvania recently decided a jurisdictional issue in favor of the buyer, stating that if a seller sells a dog in another state he should expect to have suit brought against him in that state. Thus, at least one state has decided that the sale of one dog is sufficient under the Minimal Contacts Doctrine to make the seller subject to suit in the buyer's state. In order to prevent this you should state as part of your contract that in the event of a dispute _____ (state) will have jurisdiction over the matter.

DATE AND SIGNATURES

Finally, date the agreement when it is signed and have all parties sign the agreement. If a husband and wife are involved, both should sign. Remember, dogs are property.

FINAL COMMENTS

Once you have drafted an agreement that appears to contain everything you believe should be covered, have an attorney review the final product. It is much easier for someone experienced in the law of contracts, but inexperienced in dogs, to understand and make recommendations based on the writing. In addition, it is also less expensive to have an attorney review a document than draft one.

Another good practice is to note any paragraphs that you feel are especially important and type them in boldface and have the buyer initial them to show that these, if nothing else, have been read.

CHECKLIST: MATTERS TO BE CONSIDERED
WHEN DRAFTING SALES CONTRACTS

1. Parties
   a. Names
   b. Addresses
   c. Other appropriate identification

2. Definition of terms
   a. General definitions
   b. Definition of parties
   c. Definition of subject matter of agreement
   d. Definition of nature of agreement

3. Sufficiency and effect of writing
   a. Sufficiency under Statute of Frauds
   b. Merger; writing as final expression of agreement

4. Formation of contract, offer and acceptance of terms
   a. Requisite definitiveness of terms and conditions
   b. Manner and medium of acceptance
   c. Standards for construction or interpretation

5. Description of goods

6. Modification of contract
   a. Procedures for modification
   b. Restrictions on modification

7. Obligations of parties
   a. Description of obligations or duties
   b. Effect of partial invalidity of agreement
   c. Allocation of risks between the parties
   d. Options and cooperation respecting details of performance

8. Trade terms affecting obligations of parties

9. Time for performance
    a. Limitation on time for performance
    b. Duration or termination of agreement on notice
    c. Modification of Statute of Limitations

10. Specification of price or provision for determination of price
    a. Medium of payment
    b. Tender of payment
    c. Relationship (if any) between inspection and payment

11. Delivery
    a. Identification of place of delivery
    b. Inspection at time of delivery
    c. Shipment by seller

12. Warranties
    a. Express warranties
    b. Implied warranties
    c. Disclaimer and modification of warranties

13. Title
    a. Transfer of title
    b. Reservation of security interest

14. Litigation
    a. Law to apply
    b. Alternative dispute resolution

15. Integration clause

16. Date and signatures

The above checklist applies to all contracts, not just the outright sale. Thus, some categories will not apply to all agreements. These are merely matters to be considered in drafting and need not all be contained within a given contract.

Some breeders accept deposits on future litters due to the scarcity of the breed or the puchase price. If you follow this practice it is a good idea to have a preliminary agreement, separate from the sales contract, which deals specifically with a deposit.

The bargained-for exchange (consideration) in this case is a deposit check for a guaranteed spot on a breeder's waiting list. These deposits are then deducted from the purchase price of the puppy. In the event of cancellation, the deposit is usually forfeited.

OPTION AGREEMENT

This Agreement is made this _____ day of _____, 199__, between _____ (Breeder) located at _____ and _____ (Buyer) residing at _____. The Breeder and Buyer are collectively referred to as the "parties."

The parties to this Agreement have read, understood and agreed to the terms and conditions as follows:

1. The Buyer has enclosed, with a signed copy of this Agreement, a non-refundable deposit in the amount of $_____.

2. In consideration of the Buyer's deposit, the Breeder will place the Buyer on his/her waiting list with an option to buy a _____ quality puppy from the next available litter.

    a. SHOW QUALITY is defined as a pick puppy that has the potential to be shown and titled in the conformation ring. Said puppy will be free of disqualifying faults at maturity as determined by the breed standard. Maturity is the period from 6 months of age until the dog becomes a Champion of record or two (2) years of age, whichever comes first.

    b. BREEDING QUALITY is defined as a puppy that has the potential to develop into a dog of sufficient merit so that while it may not title, it will have no genetic fault that would preclude breeding to a like or better dog.

    c. PET QUALITY is defined as a puppy that has a disqualifying fault or other shortcoming that precludes showing and/or breeding. Said fault will not prevent the puppy from living an otherwise normal and healthy life.

3. The "next available litter" is defined as a litter containing one or more _____ quality puppies as determined by the Breeder. A puppy will be offered to the Buyer based upon his/her position on the waiting list. If there are not sufficient _____ quality puppies available, the Buyer will move up on the waiting list for a subsequent litter.

4. While the final purchase price cannot be determined until the litter is evaluated, the Breeder agrees that the price shall not exceed $_____.

5. The Buyer has the option of upgrading the quality of the puppy to be purchased with the express understanding that such upgrade may delay the offer of a puppy. In the event of an upgrade, an addendum to this Agreement will be prepared and signed by all parties.

6. Upon the acceptance of an offer of a puppy, the Buyer shall sign the Sales Agreement and return it with a non-refundable partial payment of $_____ within ten (10) days of the acceptance.

7. It is expressly understood that the initial option deposit will be deducted from the final payment and not any prior partial payments.

8. Any alterations or additions to this Agreement must be in writing and signed by all parties.

9. The entire Agreement between the parties is contained
   herein.

10. In the event of a dispute, _____
    (state) will have jurisdiction over the matter.

Dated _____   _____,

                                                        Buyer

                          _____,

                                                      Breeder

6

Anatomy of a Contract II: Writing the Contingency Agreement

A CONTINGENCY or conditional contract is one where full or partial performance depends on an event, not certain to occur, which must occur.

For example, a Breeder's Term Agreement usually requires that one or more puppies be returned to the breeder of the dam as full or partial payment for the bitch. If the bitch fails to conceive, proves to be sterile or has been spayed, the contract cannot be fully performed. The same is true of the puppy-back stud fee agreement. If the bitch fails to conceive there will not be a puppy to send to the stud owner.

Technically, what you have done is to reserve a future interest in the dog you are selling under the contingency agreement. The most frequently used method of securing that interest is the co-ownership of the dog until you receive all that is due under the agreement.

Any breeder will tell you numerous horror stories about co-ownerships. However, many of the problems are due to one owner interfering with the care and training of the dog by the other. The co-ownerships that work best are those that provide only for a security interest. In addition, co-owning only to secure the future interest may alleviate a problem that is lurking somewhere over the horizon.

If a co-owned dog bites someone, the owner in possession could claim that it is a *temperament* problem originating with the breeder/co-owner. The owner not in possession could claim an environmental/training-created *behavior problem*. The courts would probably hold both parties liable, as they both own the dog. However, if you state specifically in your contract that the co-ownership is a security interest only and does not confer a present interest in the existing dog, you may be able to sidestep this issue, unless the owner can establish that it is actually a genetic temperament problem coming from your dogs' breeding.

Another factor that co-owners should be aware of is how their co-ownership will be characterized. Recently, I have seen several contracts that refer to a joint tenancy. This probably derives from an article or book, since I have seen it in a number of contracts. Be careful in using legal terms that you do not understand.

A joint tenancy is a single piece of property, real or personal, owned by two or more persons, under one instrument or act of the parties. Each owner has equal rights to share in the enjoyment of that property during their lives. Upon the death of one joint tenant, the property interest of that person descends to the surivor(s). A joint tenancy may be partitioned (divided) by one joint tenant through a sale or incumbrance without the consent of the other(s). When this happens a tenancy in common is created.

A tenancy in common is an interest in a single piece of property, real or personal, held by two or more persons having a right to possession that usually derives from a title to the same property. Each party has an undivided interest in the whole which need not be equal in size. A tenancy in common may be partitioned, sold or encumbered.

While you technically can't divide a dog into separate parts, the interests can be divided. Thus, you may find yourself with an additional owner. In addition, title to a dog is the registration certificate, which merely lists the names of the owner and co-owner(s), implying that each has an equal interest. So if you start with two owners, each having a half interest in the dog, and one party sells half of his interest, you should have two parties with a quarter interest and the third party with a half interest. However, from the paperwork it appears that three persons each have a third interest in the dog.

In order to prevent this, include a clause in your sales agreement that states specifically that neither party has the right to sell or encumber their interest in the dog prior to termination of the co-ownership.

Another pitfall in co-ownerships involves the dog's name. The American Kennel Club states that the owner has the right to name the dog and will not change it once the dog has been registered. White-out on puppy papers does not stop registrations from being regularly processed. Therefore, if the name is part of the co-ownership agreement, it is recommended that both parties agree to the registered name and sign the papers; then the seller should send them to the AKC for processing. Again, this is not a matter of mistrust, it is merely business common sense; it is important to all breeders that their puppies carry their kennel name, as one or more may rise to the top of a particular activity and be a credit and an asset to a breeding program. Protect your name.

Drafting Co-ownership Agreements

In most cases, co-ownership means a price break with a future consideration and some additional terms. The easiest way to handle this is to delete the payment clause in the body of your main contract and draft an addendum to cover each co-ownership situation. The addendum is added at the end of the primary contract and both sections are signed by all parties to the agreement.

ADDENDUM TO AGREEMENT OF SALE

The purchase price of the dog will be $_____$, payable as follows: TOTAL PRICE

a. $ _____ payable before or at the time of
   delivery;
b. First- and third-pick puppies from the bitch's first litter
   providing that there are _____ live puppies.
   Should a litter of fewer than _____ puppies result
   from the first breeding, the Seller may, at his sole discretion, delay one or both picks until a later litter of his choice.

Until the Seller receives his two (2) puppies, the bitch will be co-owned by the Seller and the Buyer. This co-ownership by the Seller is solely for the purpose of establishing a security interest in the bitch and does not obligate the Seller for any expenses incurred on behalf of the bitch. In addition, the Seller is not responsible for the action or non-action of the Buyer in housing, training and/or controlling the bitch at home or in public.

During the time that the bitch is co-owned, neither party shall have the right to sell or otherwise encumber his interest without the express written consent of the other owner.

The co-ownership shall terminate upon receipt of two puppies or at the time the bitch attains the age of six (6) years, whichever is sooner.

The selection of the stud dog shall be by mutual agreement between the Buyer and the Seller. However, the Buyer shall be responsible for the stud fee and all expenses attributable to the litter up to the point the Seller receives the two puppies and their signed registration certificates or applications.

The Seller will select his puppies no later than at _____ weeks of age. Selection will be in person, or by videotape should distance prevent personal selection. The Buyer will be responsible for any shipping costs necessary to deliver the puppies to the Seller.

Note: The TOTAL PRICE referenced above is the price for which you would have sold the dog if there were not a puppy-back agreement.

Partnership Agreements

This is becoming a more popular method of maintaining a small breeding operation. Because of number limitations in some areas and the expense related to dogs and showing, it makes good business sense to have someone else share in the operation.

Once you find a compatible person, you need to draw up a detailed agreement that sets out each person's responsibilities and financial obligations.

For example, one partner likes to train and show whereas the other prefers to raise the puppies. This frees the show partner from staying home with a litter during the show season. Both can have the part of dogs they enjoy most while reaping the benefit of the other's efforts. It is important to work out financial arrangements before entering into co-ownerships, mutual dog purchases, etc. If the expenses for each one's part generally equal out, there is no problem. However, if one party feels put upon because of spending more money than the other, the partnership can dissolve quickly and then there is the problem of dividing up the dogs.

As partnerships will vary considerably, I have not included a sample agreement, but have listed several areas that need to be addressed at the beginning.

CHECKLIST

1. Purpose of the partnership
2. Kennel name or names

45

3. Locations where dogs will be maintained; which is primary?
4. Effective date
5. Initial contribution by the partners; this need not be money, but could involve putting dogs into co-ownership
6. Purchase of assets; assumption of liabilities
7. Responsibilities of the partners to the partnership
8. Responsibility for expenses and distribution of income
9. Record-keeping requirements
10. Bank account
11. Additional partners
12. Disability of a partner
13. Withdrawal of a partner
14. Death of a partner; involuntary termination of the partnership
15. Notices
16. Amendments to partnership agreement
17. Insurance
18. Controlling law
19. Dispute resolution
20. Integration clause

While the checklist contains the essential elements of a partnership agreement, consider also the dog issues that could come into play.

1. Co-owned dogs
2. Solely owned dogs
3. Selection of stud dogs
4. Who will sell the dogs?
5. How will the dogs be named?
6. Who classifies the dogs as pet, breeding or show quality?
7. What advertising will be done and where?
8. Professional handlers—who chooses?
9. Who selects the shows to attend, minimum number per year?
10. How many litters per year?

11. Selling price of the puppies
12. Health-testing responsibilities (i.e., OFA X-rays, VWD, CERF, etc.)
13. Club memberships
14. Tournaments and special events
15. Each partner's approved spending limit for dogs, equipment, etc.
16. Distribution of dogs in the event of illness, withdrawal or death
17. If other contingency agreements are in one or both names, which partner will succeed to those future interests?
18. Maximum number of dogs
19. Selection of veterinarian(s)
20. Placement of retirees, puppies, etc.
21. Exchange/transportation of dogs—how and at whose expense?
22. Distribution of prize money, trophies and other awards
23. Minimum training required for new dogs/puppies
24. Death of a dog/necessary euthanasia
25. Minimal care requirements

7

Anatomy of a Contract III: Writing Other Agreements

THE same considerations listed in the preceding chapters apply to any other contracts you may need in dealing with your dogs and kennel. The only differences are the items pertinent to that activity that need to be included in the agreement. The following are listings of some of the items that may need to be considered for a number of agreements. Add these to the basic considerations enumerated in the prior chapters and any other items you may wish to add and contract drafting will proceed smoothly.

Stud Services

1. Stud fee? If so, when payable? Form of payment?
2. Puppy back? When selected? By whom? Option to take a stud fee payment in lieu of the puppy under certain conditions? At whose option?
3. What happens if the bitch fails to conceive? Return service? How many? When? To same male? To a different male owned by the same person? Same bitch? Different bitch? Minimum size litter? What if one of the dogs dies?

49

4. Health certificate? Brucellosis test? OFA? CERF? VWD? Vaginal culture? Sperm count?
5. Who will assume which expenses?
6. Viewing the litter: When? Personally? By a representative of the stud owner? Videotape option?
7. What happens in the event a litter is lost?
8. When will paperwork be completed? Obligation to sign? Who will send in paperwork and payment?
9. How will puppies be named? Limited registration?
10. At what point will the agreement be considered fully performed?

Additional terms need to be added in the event you decide to use new technology to effect the breeding (e.g., fresh chilled or frozen semen).

1. Are the sending and receiving veterinarians qualified for the procedure? Willing to complete the necessary paperwork?
2. Which organization's procedure will be used at both ends (e.g., ICG)?
3. Who will be responsible for the expenses of the procedure?
4. What happens if the bitch does not conceive? This is especially important when using frozen semen that originated from a dog that has since died, making access and quantity limited or impossible.
5. Any additional procedures/tests required before and/or during pregnancy?

Handling Agreements

1. Who will handle the dog? Exclusively? Handing off to an assistant? In the event of illness?
2. Term? Show-by-show basis? Monthly, annually? How many shows?

3. How are shows selected? Entry fees: up front or billed?
4. Handling fees and expenses: How calculated? When billed? Limit on total to be spent? What happens in the event of non-payment?
5. Termination clause: How can the contract be terminated? By whom? Notice requirements? Shows already entered? Return of dog?
6. Provision for care in the event of illness or in case of an emergency?
7. In the event of a dispute, who will have possession of the dog while the dispute is being resolved?
8. Photographs of wins required? Advertising required?
9. Delivery of dog to handler and return to owner: how?
10. Grooming?
11. Special care? Other specialized requirements or activities?
12. How would a breeding be handled during the term of the agreement?
13. What if dog fails to title? Time limit, show limit, etc.?
14. Indemnification of handler in the event of a bite, death of a dog, etc.?
15. Liability of the handler?
16. Record-keeping and accounting requirements?
17. Does the agreement also apply to international shows? Only those within the continental United States? Only within a specific geographical area?

Rescue/Placement Agreements

A variety of paperwork has been developed by club rescue operations. These enable the individual or committee to evaluate potential owners and their homes as well as providing a method that will maximize the potential for successful placement. Then formal agreements are signed for the protection of the dog and the rescue organization. While protection of the dog is everyone's concern, consider the potential for liability of the rescue group which has placed the dog based upon their evaluation. The implied warranty of fitness for the general purpose of a dog as a companion animal will apply here as well as to a breeder.

1. Purpose of placement?
2. Home inspections: Initial? Continuing?
3. Minimal housing requirements? Care requirements?
4. Full disclosure of temperament and behavior of dog: Who evaluated? For how long? By any specific method?
5. Special care required?
6. Indemnification of rescue group by new owner in case of an incident.
7. Donation, if any, to the rescue organization?
8. What happens if the dog does not work out? If the owner cannot keep the dog for life?
9. Neutering requirements? Reimbursement if done prior to placement?
10. Notification requirements (e.g., in the event owner moves, new rescue chairperson, etc.)?
11. Who would be authorized to terminate a placement?
12. Who is authorized to sign agreements in the name of the club or rescue group?

Service Dog Organizations

Service dog organizations require a number of agreements, including, but not necessarily limited to, (1) puppy/adult donation agreement, (2) puppy home or foster/training home agreement and (3) placement agreement. Many of these issues are complex and should be professionally drafted for this highly specialized function.

8

Enforcing the Contract

WHILE written agreements are designed to prevent misunderstandings and avoid the necessity for legal action, not every contractual relationship functions perfectly and disputes do arise for a variety of reasons.

When this happens the first task is to determine exactly what the problem is, what caused it and what needs to be done to resolve the situation.

Before instituting legal action, consider if there is an alternative method to resolving the dispute. Can an impartial third party arbitrate or mediate the problem? Will the intervention of an attorney resolve it without resort to the courts? In many cases there has been a breakdown in communication that can be remedied outside the legal system. If, however, you have tried everything you can think of to find a resolution, then you may have to consider legal action.

While a contract will often resolve itself upon a thorough reading of those clauses applicable to a given situation, sometimes you are left with no other choice but to sue or be sued.

Depending upon the situation, you can seek money damages in a court of law or seek specific performance under the contract in a court of equity. However, access to the equity system is limited to those situations where money damages are insufficient to make the plaintiff whole again. The argument that dog cases should be heard in equity is that a given dog is a unique piece of property and no money, no matter how great, will compensate the plaintiff; only the actual dog will suffice.

Though the court systems vary from state to state, and even sometimes from county to county within a state, most have a number of lower courts of limited jurisdiction based upon the amount of damages claimed. For example, New Jersey has a Small Claims division, a Special Civil Part and the Superior Court. Small Claims has reasonable filing fees and you don't necessarily need an attorney to file or represent you in court. The disadvantage is that the defendant does not have to answer the complaint; he must only appear on the day scheduled. Thus you do not know what his defense will be and which witnesses you should have on hand. As both parties must appear, if the plaintiff fails to show up the matter is dismissed; if the defendant fails to appear then a judgment is given the plaintiff. These courts handle a multitude of matters and you might as well plan to spend the day.

A Special Civil Part division is a step above the Small Claims situation. While filing fees are higher, so is the jurisdictional dollar limit. In addition, the defendant must answer the complaint or be subject to a default judgment for the plaintiff. You will only need to appear if an answer to your complaint has been filed. Again, plan to spend the day.

Small Claims and Special Civil Part are usually handled by the same court clerks who are used to dealing with private individuals who wish to pursue their own actions (pro se) and are knowledgeable and willing to assist you.

Now the real question is: Is it worth it to initiate legal action? That depends on what you are trying to accomplish. As noted earlier, money awards in dog cases are low. It may cost you more in fees than you will ultimately be awarded. Also consider how important the issue is to you and/or other dog people. There are some situations that simply need to be pursued and, if the proper case arises, should be fully litigated (e.g., whether or not a lemon law should apply to private breeders). If you have the finances and are willing to settle for personal satisfaction you may want to pursue certain matters. However, there are some areas where personal satisfaction will be limited to simply winning, as the defendants are insured, litigation will be handled by attorneys for the insurance companies and any money you receive will be paid by the insurance. Little damage will be caused the defendants; most will still be in business. So carefully consider what you are really after before taking further steps.

If you do decide to take legal action or if it should be instituted against you in any form, get an attorney. In the past most dog people could handle their own business in the lower courts. Today, the law pertaining to dog cases is in such a state of flux, with the attendant hostility of many people against dogs and their owners, that having experienced legal counsel with you is a prudent step.

9

Protecting Dogs
in the Event of . . .

TRAGEDY can strike at any time. An unexpected emergency can leave those depending upon you at loose ends. This is especially true for single dog owners who have not set up a backup system.

This is not an unusual situation. Most people put off drawing up a will until something happens that scares them into the process. So why should these same people think about arranging for their pets' future when they are already failing to put their affairs in sufficient order to make life a little easier for those left behind?

There has been considerable grousing about the AKC's crackdown on record-keeping requirements. However, the underlying reason for the uniformity and constant upkeep of paperwork makes sense. The basic premise behind these requirements is that a complete stranger can come onto your property and through your records identify each dog. This only makes good sense for any multiple dog owner should the situation arise that you are unable to return to your kennel for an extended period of time.

In Case of an Accident

Most dog people travel a great deal. The more miles you cover, the greater the risk of an accident. This may occur some distance from your home where few people, if any, know you or your dogs.

When driving, your first precaution should be to either crate your dogs or secure them behind a barrier, away from the passenger compartment. Crating is preferred because it is more secure—especially if you are rendered unconscious and require outside aid. Any dog, regardless of its size, will protect its owner from a perceived threat. Strangers attempting to enter a vehicle to remove the driver will be perceived as a threat. Emergency personnel and law enforcement officials will take whatever action is necessary to reach the human occupant. This may include shooting your dogs while they are in the process of protecting you.

Now, assuming the dogs are safely confined and you are receiving medical attention, what happens to the dogs still in the vehicle? That depends on you. It is a simple matter to leave instructions for the professionals at the scene of an accident. List one or more persons with name, address and phone number who will be responsible for collecting your dogs. Request that any injured dogs be taken to a reputable veterinarian and that any uninjured dogs be boarded at the vet's or in a reputable kennel. Be sure to state that all expenses will be guaranteed by the person who will take possession of the dogs. List your regular veterinarian's name and phone number and ask that he be contacted regarding treatment of the dogs, if possible. As if you are drafting a living will for yourself, state at what point you want a dog humanely euthanized. Be specific and include all the variables you wish to have considered in making that decision.

Always carry photos and a list by call name of all the dogs traveling with you. In the event a dog has gotten loose during or following an accident, the personnel at the scene will need to know that there is a missing dog and, once located, be able to identify the dog as yours. Also, carry copies of health records, rabies certificates and details of any special condition of any dog. Date, sign and have notarized a number of copies.

In all the emergency information, stress that time is of the essence and that the care of your animals should take place without delay. If they are show dogs, state that fact and stress that they are valuable, well socialized and capable of being handled without tranquilizers or restraints. While these methods may still be used as safety precautions, people are more willing to start assisting a dog that is friendly and well trained. This is especially true if you have large, intimidating-looking dogs. Also include a brief write-up of your breed for the veterinarian or boarding kennel in case they have never heard of or seen the breed before.

Finally, distribute several copies of this information throughout the vehicle (e.g., glove compartment, purse or carryall, taped in the back with the dogs). Mark each packet clearly in large letters: "EMERGENCY DOG INFORMA-TION—OPEN AND READ IMMEDIATELY!"

In Case of an Emergency

We have all heard that most accidents happen in the home or within fifteen miles thereof. In most cases you will not have a dog with you, but there are those left at home to be concerned about should you be unable to return or call for assistance.

As with long-distance travel, leave a note in a conspicuous place stating that you have animals at home that require attention in the event you are injured and unable to communicate. Leave names and phone numbers that can be called.

Emergencies in the home are more difficult to prepare for before they occur. If you work, co-workers should be aware of your dogs and directed to contact someone should you fail to appear and cannot be contacted. If you have family in the area, they should be made aware of what to do with the dogs and whom to contact in case there is a problem. Neighbors and friends can also be put on call just in case. A friendly neighbor can be especially valuable, as many dogs will set up quite a racket if a problem occurs with their owner at home. A neighbor who knows the usual routine at your home will notice if something is awry.

Another good idea is to post stickers on all openings to your dwelling alerting emergency personnel that there are pets present. Also note the location of instructions for their care and the names and phone numbers of those who will care for your animals in your absence.

'Til Death Do Us Part

What would happen to your animals if you died suddenly? Sadly, it may mean a quick trip to the vet's office if you haven't made provisions for their placement and care.

There are two types of prior arrangements that can be made: formal and informal.

Informal arrangements are much like those described for accidents or emergencies. However, remember that there will be an estate and paperwork problems that you should address beforehand.

More formal arrangements contained in a will or a letter of instruction attached to the will are probably the better solution. However, remember that dogs are property and cannot inherit directly under your will. On the other hand, someone can inherit your dogs who may not be the best person to do so. Most wills provide for the disposition of the residual estate, that remaining after all other expenses, claims and bequests have been paid. If there is no specific provision for the dogs they may become part of that residual estate. If the person you leave the residual estate to is your eighty-three-year-old Aunt May, who lives in a one-bedroom apartment in a town with a one-dog limit, there may be a problem with your eight Rottweilers, three Great Danes and five Chihuahuas tagging along with the $500 left in your estate.

There are various methods that can be used to provide for your dogs in the event of your death. You can leave them and money for their continued care to one person; you can leave the dogs to one person and the money for their care to a second person. The easiest, of course, is to involve one individual who has already agreed to take the dogs and whom you trust to do what is best—keep, place or euthanize. However, leaving the dogs to one person and money to another can work, but in the event of a change in circumstances you must remember to change your will. For example, if the dogs go to person A and $5,000 goes to person B and the dog dies before you, then person A does not have the dog but person B still gets the $5,000 without any obligation to person A.

Trusts are another method of providing for your dogs. However, since a dog is property it cannot be the direct beneficiary of a trust. In that situation, the trustee would have no obligation to carry out the trust, as the dog is not a legal beneficiary. However, the courts often prefer to characterize it as an "honorary trust" to give effect to the decedent's intent. However, not all courts are animal-friendly and some have a problem when called upon to suspend the transfer of an interest in an estate to a human in order to benefit a non-human.

Finally, one of the best methods, allowed in some states, is the letter of instruction that is attached to the will. This can be changed easily and will operate to immediately allow the person involved to deal with the dogs and their care.

TO MY FAMILY AND FRIENDS
It is my wish that, in the event of my death, any and all dogs in my possession be given to Jane Doe. She, at her sole discretion, will keep, place or have these animals humanely euthanized.

or,

TO MY FAMILY AND FRIENDS
It is my wish that, in the event of my death, dogs
A and B be given Jane Doe and dogs C, D and E
be given to John James.

Conclusion

While this is not an easy or pleasant subject to deal with, it
is one each of us needs to consider. Do make the effort and
insist that your attorney take your concerns regarding the
future welfare of your dogs seriously.

10

Veterinary Practice and Malpractice

A VETERINARIAN you can trust and communicate with is your and your dog's best friend. Once you find a vet that you can establish a workable relationship with, you will stay with him/her as long as possible. Over the years there will be a number of little mistakes that will be overlooked, as they should be, because we are all only human.

The real horror stories of the veterinary profession are relatively rare. Most problems occur when you are consulting a specialist or trying to find a new practice in an unfamiliar area. You do not have the established relationship with that vet or practice and communication breaks down, doesn't occur at all or you and the doctor are not on the same level. This is happening more and more because of the increase in specialization in veterinary medicine. New and improved technologies have made it virtually impossible for the general practitioner to keep up with every area of practice.

While professional and semi-professional dog people have developed a network of specialists over the years, the less sophisticated dog owner is at a distinct disadvantage, especially in more remote areas. Thus you may have to make some concessions to a veterinarian's personality and communication methods, as vets do not have a duty to treat any animal presented to them. However, if they undertake treatment they cannot stop it if the animal still requires their services for a specific condition.

If you have a choice in the matter, select the vet whom you feel you can establish a workable relationship with. If not, then monitor the treatment and question anything you don't understand and keep questioning until you get understandable answers. You have a right to know your dog's diagnosis, treatment protocol and prognosis. Veterinarians are licensed by the state or states in which they practice, are subject to discipline and can be sued for malpractice.

A veterinarian will be held to a higher standard of care than a technician, an assistant or a dog owner. Because of his/her special education and experience the standard is that of a reasonable veterinarian. In some states this will mean another veterinarian in the same community whereas in others it will mean one similarly situated. As numbers of specialists continue to increase, there will be an even higher standard applied to them, as they have had additional education, training and experience in a specific area.

If something goes wrong, the question becomes whether it falls into the malpractice category or that of simple negligence.

Negligence is the failure to exercise the degree of care which a reasonable person would exercise under the same circumstances. Malpractice, on the other hand, is a professional's failure to exercise the degree of care which a professional similarly situated would have exercised in a professional relationship of like circumstances with his client.

The veterinarian may also be liable for the conduct of his employees when they are treating/handling the dogs. As the professional, he is the responsible party and must provide sufficient training and supervision to anyone assisting him in the practice.

However, whether or not a given event constitutes malpractice, you may not want to institute litigation because the probability of recovery or the recovery itself is low. Rather, you can report the matter to the licensing agency for investigation. It all depends upon what you are seeking to accomplish.

Like medical doctors, more and more veterinarians are facing malpractice allegations. These will only serve to increase the costs of their services as insurance rates skyrocket. Learning from what has happened in human medicine, we, the clients, can help keep costs down by becoming educated consumers. We can take steps to evaluate the practice before becoming clients, changing if we are not satisfied with the services, asking questions regarding treatment and refusing specific procedures until we can seek a second opinion or find a specialist in that area of practice.

There are a variety of things that can happen at the veterinarian's office that could be considered malpractice and only an attorney can evaluate the specific situation and advise you as to what, if any, action to take. However, don't expect your attorney to take the case on a contingency basis, in which he takes a certain percentage of the final settlement or award, but only if the matter is settled or he wins at trial and collects. This type of litigation can be expensive, especially when expert witnesses are required and have to be paid for their time.

On the other hand, you will not be liable to the veterinarian if your dog bites him or his employees. The possibility of a dog bite is part of the risk of being in that profession. The vet and his employees should know how to properly and safely handle dogs who are sick or injured. Since he has voluntarily exposed himself to that risk, he cannot hold the owner liable for any resulting injury. However, if the owner of a dog coming to the practice for the first time knows or should have known of the dog's tendency to bite in that situation or generally and did not so inform the vet, the owner could be liable for the resulting injury. But if the owner advises the vet of that known propensity and the vet undertakes to treat the dog anyway, the owner is relieved of liability should the dog bite.

A final comment needs to be made regarding consent forms you will be presented with from time to time. These are comparable to those you would sign in a hospital and your consent should be equally informed at either location. Read these carefully before you sign and ask questions if you don't understand something. If the standard form does not express in clear, understandable terms what you and the veterinarian have agreed to, ask that this be done before you sign. While some of the basic consent clauses, probably drafted by the practice's attorney, will not be subject to modification, most veterinarians will readily agree to additions so that there will be no misunderstanding. If they refuse, unless you are in an emergency situation where you have no choice, find another practice.

Modern Technology

Veterinary medicine has come a long way since I was first involved with dogs. These advances have created a whole new set of considerations for the dog owner as well as the veterinarian.

The first question is when is enough enough. There comes a point when the owner, in consultation with the veterinarian, has to decide whether or not treatment should continue or when the latest procedure is not going to be sufficiently beneficial to the animal. It is too easy to get caried away with the latest developments and forget the dog involved.

While a person can make a living will that will determine at what point he does not want further medical interference, a dog cannot do the same. However, the owner should make clear to the veterinarian what his wishes are and obtain his consent beforehand.

Another consideration is how fully should you warranty your puppies in light of veterinary advances. In the past, hip dysplasia warranties were based upon the assumption that little could be done other than to relieve discomfort caused by the condition or put the dog down. Today, there are numerous surgical procedures that may or may not remedy the problem. Combine this with potential lemon laws and we could be held liable for the cost of hip replacements.

Finally, does the veterinarian have the right to interfere with our relationship with the breeder/trainer, etc.? And if so, to what degree?

Recently, I have seen a number of situations where veterinarians write letters to breeders advising them about problems with their lines and recommending that they not breed these dogs. Also, some vets will recommend that the owner contact consumer affairs about the situation. What has happened to the recommendation that the owner contact the breeder first? Then, if the problem cannot be resolved, there are other avenues of assistance the owner can pursue. Also, should the general practice veterinarian be so eager to make these kinds of decisions in areas that have become highly specialized?

These are evolving issues raised by the rapid advances in veterinary medicine. In the not so distant future, standard methods of handling a variety of situations will undoubtedly develop.

Practice of Veterinary Medicine Without a License

A frequently asked question is: What exactly constitutes practicing veterinary medicine without a license? Can I whelp someone else's litter? Can I condition dogs for the show ring for another owner? Can I give my puppies their shots?

As veterinarians are licensed under a state statutory scheme, you should check that in your own state. However, generally, you can do just about anything you wish to your own dogs, those you own or co-own, without a problem. However, any procedure or service performed on someone else's dogs would be practicing veterinary medicine without a license and not only would subject you to problems with the licensing authority but could leave you open to substantial liability. This would not be true if you are doing so under the supervision of a veterinarian. However, in that situation the veterinarian has the ultimate reponsibility.

11

Property Damage

Nuisance

A nuisance is anything that interferes with the free use and enjoyment of one's property. It extends to anything that endangers health or safety, offends the senses or obstructs the reasonable and comfortable use of one's property. The nuisance itself originates from the unreasonable or unlawful use of property to the discomfort, annoyance, inconvenience or damage to another.

Nuisances are divided into two broad categories—public and private. A public nuisance is the unreasonable interference with a right common to the general public. It comprises behavior that unreasonably interferes with the health, safety, peace, comfort or convenience of the general community. It offends the public at large or a segment of the public. A private nuisance is an interference with a person's interest in the private use and enjoyment of his property. It offends only a particular person or persons.

Various acts of dogs and dog owners can constitute a private and/or public nuisance. For example, barking that is continuous or recurrent could be either. The odor coming from a kennel that is not cleaned regularly could be either.

The closer you live to your neighbors, the more careful you will have to be in controlling your dogs. Claiming that your dogs are a nuisance is the most frequent charge leveled by an unfriendly neighbor.

Dogs can also constitute an attractive nuisance—namely, a dangerous instrumentality on the premises that is likely to attract children and puts the owner under a duty to reasonably protect those children against that attraction. You may not consider your dogs either dangerous or likely to attract children. However, liability can be based on nothing more than foreseeable harm to a child as well as the social policies that work to bring a balance between the conflicting interests of an individual's right to act and public safety. So while your dogs may not be dangerous in most situations, it takes just one incident to bring about liability. You cannot rely on parents to control their children; nor will the courts do more than consider that the child was a trespasser on your property. You are better off assuming that children are attracted to dogs and protecting your dogs and yourself from potential problems.

Condo Commandos *vs.* The Dog Owner

About thirty years ago someone had a brilliant idea, one that was destined to change the way thousands of people lived. The idea was to design a community that would be attractive and self-contained and have the means by which it would retain its look and appeal over time. Thus was the Planned Unit Development concept born.

While there are many variations on this theme, none of them are dog-friendly. All of them maximize the number of people per acre of land.

The least restrictive is the single-family home development. Since they are detached units, there is some land around the dwelling. There will undoubtedly be some form of restriction (e.g., a two-dog/pet limit) but a total ban is unlikely. Each of these homes is individually owned, as is the land. There are no common areas other than municipal property that is maintained by tax dollars. No fees are paid to an association. Any damage the dog does to the owner's property is the owner's problem and no one else's unless a health violation/problem exists. Usually the municipality will have minimum standards for your home and property and as long as these are complied with there should not be a problem. You may have your animals within these limits.

Another type of community is the townhouse development. These are usually governed by an association, which charges monthly fees for the maintenance of common ground. All the units are individually owned. In some units you also own the land beneath the unit and in others you also own a front and back yard. Common ground is any property owned by the association members as a group (e.g., open field, pools, etc.). Depending upon the age of the community and what is contained in the governing documents, the local municipal regulations may apply unless the association has independent authority to set rules and regulations combined with the ability to levy fines or otherwise enforce them.

Probably the worst type of community for the dog owner is the condominium. As this type of development is becoming more and more popular, there is reason to be concerned. Here the owner owns the interior of the unit up to the points set forth in the master deed and bylaws. Everthing else is common property and must be maintained, repaired or replaced by the association through monthly fee assessments and any other special assessments that may be necessary. Furthermore, the board of trustees is given the authority to set rules and regulations as well as the ability to fine and enforce these rules. The common ground is where the problem occurs. Fees are high, and landscaping is done regularly and well. Thus any destruction to the land or landscaping is the responsibility of everyone. That a few owners with dogs can incur costs for the many is considered unfair and boards are passing rules against dogs in the community, often after the fact, where dogs living there already are allowed to remain but cannot be replaced. To date these prohibitions have stood.

Specialized communities for dog and horse owners have been successful. However, they are too few and far between to be a viable alternative today.

Overall, the denser the community and the more common ground there is, the more potential there is for conflict. These are highly diversified groups of people whose only commonality is the choice of that community location and type and incomes that can support that style of living.

People Injuring/Killing Dogs

Generally you may do whatever is necessary to stop a dog from attacking a person or livestock. If this includes injuring or even killing the dog, you will not be liable to the owner. Some statutes use the term "worrying" to extend the right to take action even when there is not an actual attack. Actions constituting worrying of livestock would include barking, chasing or frightening.

The dog, however, must usually be caught in the act and can only be stopped on the farmer/rancher's own property. You usually are not authorized to track the dog back to its home and shoot it there—though a few statutes do allow pursuit in somewhat the same way police are allowed to cross jurisdictional lines when in "hot pursuit."

What is so difficult in this area is the variety of specific inclusions and exclusions on local, county and state levels. While you can stop a dog attacking livestock you may not be allowed to do so if it is attacking another dog. While dog fighting is illegal and efforts are being made to stop the activity, it is the activity overall that is illegal, constituting cruelty to animals, not necessarily one dog attacking another.

Many of these statutes are drafted broadly. In one location

your dog may kill a cat that trespasses onto your property without liability while in another the mere act of attacking and/or killing may create a vicious dog problem as well as subject you to liability for the cat.

The only general area where a dog owner would have a claim for damages is when someone intentionally or through carelessness injures or kills a dog.

12

Legislative Action

MOST legislation is the result of a perceived need or overt public pressure. While often well intentioned, lawmakers rarely have the kind of detailed information and/ or experience needed to effectively draft, debate and enact fair and reasonable dog laws.

Legislation impacts in three areas: protecting the public from the big, bad dogs, protecting the consumer from the big, bad breeders, and protecting the dogs from the big, bad people.

Vicious Dog Laws

Vicious dog laws, breed-specific or not, have proliferated throughout this country at an unprecedented rate. While most licensing or other animal control ordinances that had already been in place provided some method for dealing with dog bites and, especially, repeat offenders, the current rash of hastily drafted proposals have gone overboard.

Early ordinances often allowed for the "one bite" rule, whereby a dog would not be considered vicious until he had bitten one person in an unprovoked situation. An extension of the "one bite" rule was the "known propensity" standard of liability. If a dog had bitten once, the owner was presumed to know that the dog had the propensity to bite. Therefore, he should take extra precautions to effectively control the dog so that there would not be a second bite. However, a dog could have a "known propensity" toward biting that the owner should or did know of based upon the dog's past actions whether or not they resulted in a bite. If the owner knew, or should have known, that the dog had the propensity, he would be liable. One bite already taken would be considered "prima facie" evidence (evidence on its face) that the owner knew of the dog's propensity, and a second bite would result in liability.

New Jersey, which now has one of the best non-breed-specific vicious dog laws, took the liability issue to an extreme. In a case that held sway for many years a strict liability standard had been enunciated by the judge: "All dogs have teeth, therefore all dogs can bite. Thus, if your dog bites, you are liable" (to the injured party). There were no exceptions, regardless of the situation or the relationship between the parties. The original case involved a suit brought by a child's parents against the grandparents!

Over the years, other persons, in addition to those who owned or had possession and control of the dog, have been brought into lawsuits arising from dog bites. The landlord is a favorite target and many courts have held him liable under the "known propensity" standard. As most apartment dwellings are private property, the landlord owes a duty to the tenants and those others who are legally upon the property to maintain a safe environment. If the landlord knows or should have known of the dog's propensity to bite, he has breached the duty and is liable for the injury caused by his negligence in not abating the unsafe condition. Aside from concerns about property destruction, it is little wonder that landlords do not usually allow dogs to live on their property.

Thus the problem of dogs injuring people has always been

there and has been handled in a variety of ways. However, once the "pit bull" scare took hold, these primary ordinances were perceived as insufficient to handle a danger of this magnitude. Thus new laws were quickly drafted and enacted. Most were defeated due to their vagueness in determining if a dog is or is not a pit bull. This gave the dog world time to marshal their forces, since we, as a group, had been blindsided by the whole series of events. For the first time in their history, the American Kennel Club and the United Kennel Club made a concerted effort against a mutual threat. The American Dog Owners' Association has spearheaded many of the efforts to date and maintains a war chest to fight other inappropriate legislation directly affecting our dogs. More recently, the American Kennel Club has set up a hot line for the reporting of all enacted and pending legislation throughout the country. The AKC has also asked each club to designate a legislative liaison to the AKC. A number of local groups have been organized in order to monitor and fight inappropriate laws. However, with all this effort, there are still many problems out there and more on the way.

First let's examine a vicious dog law that has been cited as a good example. While this New Jersey statute is not necessarily model legislation, it has dealt innovatively with problems faced by other jurisdictions. Though it did not start out that way, through the concerted efforts of the New Jersey Federation of Dog Clubs and many individuals, the bill enacted has been used as a model by other states. It is not perfect, but several points are important.

Read the following thoroughly while paying attention to the language used. Language is extremely important in any legal document and can make the difference between good, indifferent or detrimental effects. Also, pay special attention to the Governor's Recommendation Statement and the enforcement provisions.

4:19–17. Legislative findings and declarations

The Legislature finds and declares that certain dogs are an increasingly serious and widespread threat to the safety and welfare of citizens of this State by virtue of their unprovoked attacks on, and associated injury to, individuals and other animals; that these attacks are in part attributable to the failure of owners to confine and properly train and control these dogs; that existing laws at the local level inadequately address this problem; and that it is therefore appropriate and necessary to impose a uniform set of State requirements on the owners of vicious or potentially dangerous dogs.

L.1989, c. 307, § 1, eff. Jan. 12, 1990.

Governor's Reconsideration and Recommendation Statement

Senate Bill No. 3276—L.1989, c. 307

To the Senate:

Pursuant to Article V, Section I, Paragraph 14 of the Constitution, I am returning Senate Bill No. 3276 (Second Reprint) with my objections for reconsideration.

The purpose of this bill is to provide a uniform Statewide approach to the serious and widespread threat that unprovoked dog attacks pose to the safety and welfare of our citizens. Recognizing that dog attacks are, in part, attributable to the failure of owners to confine and properly train and control their dogs, as well as the inadequacy of local laws addressing these concerns, this bill proposes a comprehensive scheme directed toward ascertaining whether a dog is "vicious" or "potentially dangerous." It also prescribes various requirements for dogs that are found to be vicious or potentially dangerous, ranging from humane destruction to mandatory licensure of such dogs.

Specifically, this legislation authorizes municipal animal control officers to seize and impound a dog when an officer has reasonable cause to believe that the animal is either responsible for an unprovoked attack or has been trained or encouraged to engage in unprovoked attacks. It also mandates that the chief law enforcement or health officer of each municipality empanel three "qualified individuals" from a group encompassing veterinarians, dog breeders, professional dog handlers and obedience trainers or animal behavioralists to determine whether a dog is vicious or potentially dangerous. If, following the exhaustion of all appeals as set forth in the Act, a dog is deemed "vicious," this bill mandates that such dog be destroyed in a humane and expeditious manner. Similarly, if a dog is deemed to be "potentially dangerous," various requirements including, among other things, licensure and registration with both the appropriate municipality and the Department of Health, are imposed as conditions of continued ownership of that dog. Finally, this legislation appropriates $85,000 from the General Fund to the Department of Health to implement the provisions of this Act.

While I strongly support the intent of this initiative, sound policy, combined with present fiscal constraints, prevent me from endorsing this bill in its present form. My objections, however, should not be construed as a dissent from the Legislature's sound conclusion that a uniform Statewide program is essential to ameliorate both the threat and reality of unprovoked dog attacks. However, I am convinced that the progressive agenda embarked upon in this legislation can be effectively achieved through diligent and responsible administration at the municipal level, without the need to involve the Department of Health and the concomitant depletion of General Fund resources.

In particular, I see no profit in requiring the Department of Health to issue each "potentially dangerous" dog a registration number and identification tag in addition to the special municipal license required to be used for potentially dangerous dogs. Rather, I believe the Department should be required to establish regulations creating a registry system to be utilized by the municipalities. Each municipality will be assigned a three-number code that will be the last three digits of every potentially dangerous dog license and registration number issued by that municipality. Through this coding system, the name of the issuing municipality could be quickly identified and the municipality could then be contacted for specific information regarding the dog or its owner. Further, the other tasks assigned by this legislation to the Department of Health will provide no additional safeguards to the public and can be eliminated without any significant impact on the overall effort to control vicious and potentially dangerous dogs.

Since I am confident that the objectives of this legislation can be accomplished without involving the Department of Health and without the commitment of General Fund resources, I herewith return Senate Bill No. 3276 (Second Reprint) and recommend that it be amended as follows:

[Recommendations by Governor are incorporated in the bill as enacted]

* * * *

Respectfully,
/s/ Thomas H. Kean
GOVERNOR

4:19–18. Definitions

As used in this act:

"Animal control officer" means a certified municipal animal control officer or, in the absence of such an officer, the chief law enforcement officer of the municipality or his designee.

"Department" means the Department of Health.

"Dog" means any dog or dog hybrid.

"Domestic animal" means any cat, dog, or livestock other than poultry.

"Panel" means any panel selected pursuant to section 5 of this act.[1]

"Potentially dangerous dog" means any dog or dog hybrid declared potentially dangerous by the panel pursuant to section 7 of this act.[2]

"Vicious dog" means any dog or dog hybrid declared vicious by the panel pursuant to section 6 of this act.[3]

L.1989, c. 307, § 2, eff. Jan. 12, 1990.

[1] Section 4:19–21.
[2] Section 4:19–23.
[3] Section 4:19–22.

4:19–19. Seizure and impoundment of dog by animal control officer; grounds

An animal control officer shall seize and impound a dog when the officer has reasonable cause to believe that the dog:

a. attacked a person and caused death or serious bodily injury as defined in N.J.S. 2C:11–1(b) to that person;

b. caused bodily injury as defined in N.J.S.2C:11–1(a) to a person during an unprovoked attack and poses a serious threat of harm to persons or domestic animals;

c. engaged in dog fighting activities as described in R.S.4:22–24 and R.S.4:22–26; or

d. has been trained, tormented, badgered, baited or encouraged to engage in unprovoked attacks upon persons or domestic animals.

The dog shall be impounded until the final disposition as to whether the dog is vicious or potentially dangerous. Subject to the approval of the municipal health officer, the dog may be impounded in a facility or other structure agreeable to the owner.

L.1989, c. 307, § 3, eff. Jan. 12, 1990.

4:19-20. Notice of seizure and impoundment; determination of identity of owner; notice of hearing; return of statement by owner; destruction of dog

a. The animal control officer shall notify the official responsible for convening a hearing pursuant to section 5 and the municipal health officer within three working days that he has seized and impounded a dog pursuant to section 3 of this act,[1] or that he has reasonable cause to believe that a dog has killed another domestic animal and that a hearing is required. The animal control officer shall through a reasonable effort attempt to determine the identity of the owner of any dog seized and impounded. If its owner cannot be identified within seven days, that dog may be humanely destroyed.

b. The official responsible for convening a hearing pursuant to section 5 of this act[2] shall, within three working days of the determination of the identity of the owner of a dog seized and impounded pursuant to this act, notify by certified mail, return receipt requested the owner concerning the seizure and impoundment and the grounds for a hearing pursuant to section 5. This notice shall also require that the owner return within seven days, by certified mail or hand delivery, a signed statement indicating whether he wishes the hearing to be conducted or, if not, to relinquish ownership of the dog, in which case the dog may be humanely destroyed. If the owner cannot be notified by certified mail, return receipt requested, or refuses to sign for the certified letter, or does not reply to the certified letter with a signed statement within seven days of receipt, the dog may be humanely destroyed.

L.1989, c. 307, § 4, eff. Jan. 12, 1990.

1 Section 4:19-19.
2 Section 4:19-21.

4:19-21. Hearing; panel; selection; notice to owner; presentation of evidence

a. The chief law enforcement officer of the municipality or the municipal health officer shall select a panel of three qualified individuals knowledgeable about dog behavior and conduct a hearing, within 30 days of the receipt of the signed statement from the dog's owner as required by subsection b. of section 4 of this act,[1] to determine whether the dog impounded pursuant to section 3 of this act[2] is vicious or potentially dangerous. In no case may the municipal official who is the supervisor of the animal control officer presenting the case select the panel. If neither the chief law enforcement officer of the municipality nor the municipal health officer is the animal control officer's supervisor, the municipal health officer shall select the panel and conduct the hearing. To the greatest extent practicable, the selected panel shall collectively represent a diverse background in dog behavior and in no case may all of the members of the panel be from the same discipline nor may a panel include any individual connected to the case. Upon request, the department may recommend to the municipal health officer or chief law enforcement officer of the municipality the names of qualified individuals to serve on the panel. For the purposes of this section, "qualified individuals" means:

(1) veterinarians specializing in the treatment of dogs and cats;

(2) American Kennel Club certified dog breed or obedience judges;

(3) professional dog handlers who are members of the Professional Handlers Association or who are recommended by either a Professional Handlers Association member or an American Kennel Club certified dog breed judge;

(4) professional dog obedience trainers who are members of the National Association of Dog Obedience Instructors or who are recommended by a National Association of Dog Obedience Instructors member or an American Kennel Club dog obedience judge;

(5) dog behavior modification trainers who are recommended by a veterinarian specializing in the treatment of dogs and cats, an American Kennel Club dog obedience judge, a National Association of Dog Obedience Instructors member or persons in paragraph (6) below; or

(6) animal behaviorists with at least a bachelor's degree in animal behavior specializing in the treatment of canine behavior disorders.

b. The official conducting the hearing shall notify the owner of the impounded dog by certified mail, return receipt requested, and the department of the date and time of the hearing, and the names of the panel members selected. During the hearing, the owner shall have the opportunity to present evidence to demonstrate that the dog is not vicious or potentially dangerous.

L.1989, c. 307, § 5, eff. Jan. 12, 1990.

1 Section 4:19–20.
2 Section 4:19–19.

4:19–22. Finding to declare dog vicious; grounds

a. The panel shall declare the dog vicious if it finds by a preponderance of the evidence that the dog:

(1) killed a person or caused serious bodily injury as defined in N.J.S.2C:11–1(b) to a person; or

(2) has engaged in dog fighting activities as described in R.S.4:22–24 and R.S.4:22–26.

b. A dog may not be declared vicious for inflicting death or serious bodily injury as defined in N.J.S.2C:11–1(b) upon a person if that person was committing or attempting to commit a crime or if that person was tormenting or inflicting pain upon the dog in such an extreme manner that an attack of such nature could be considered provoked.

c. If the panel declares a dog to be vicious, and no appeal is made of this ruling pursuant to subsection c. of section 9 of this act,[1] the dog shall be destroyed in a humane and expeditious manner, except that no dog may be destroyed during the pendency of an appeal.

L.1989, c. 307, § 6, eff. Jan. 12, 1990.

1 Section 4:19–25.

4:19–23. Finding to declare dog potentially dangerous

a. The panel shall declare a dog to be potentially dangerous if it finds that the dog:

(1) caused bodily injury as defined in N.J.S.2C:11–1(a) to a person during an unprovoked attack, and poses a serious threat of bodily injury or death to a person, or

(2) killed another domestic animal, and

(a) poses a threat of serious bodily injury or death to a person; or

(b) poses a threat of death to another domestic animal, or

(3) has been trained, tormented, badgered, baited or encouraged to engage in unprovoked attacks upon persons or domestic animals.

b. A dog shall not be declared potentially dangerous for:

(1) causing bodily injury as defined in N.J.S.2C:11–1(a) to a person if that person was committing or attempting to commit a crime or if that person was tormenting or inflicting pain upon the dog in such an extreme manner that an attack of such nature could be considered provoked, or

(2) killing a domestic animal if the domestic animal was the aggressor.

L.1989, c. 307, § 7, eff. Jan. 12, 1990.

4:19–24. Order and schedule for compliance for potentially dangerous dog; conditions

If the panel declares the dog to be potentially dangerous, it shall issue an order and a schedule for compliance which, in part:

a. shall require the owner to comply with the following conditions:

(1) to apply, at his own expense, to the municipal clerk or other official designated to license dogs pursuant to section 2 of P.L.1941, c. 151 (C.4:19–15.2), for a special municipal potentially dangerous dog license, municipal registration number, and red identification tag issued pursuant to section 14 of this act.[1] The owner shall, at his own expense, have the registration number tattooed upon the dog in a prominent location. A potentially dangerous dog shall be impounded until the owner obtains a municipal potentially dangerous dog license, municipal registration number, and red identification tag;

(2) to display, in a conspicuous manner, a sign on his premises warning that a potentially dangerous dog is on the premises. The sign shall be visible and legible from 50 feet of the enclosure required pursuant to paragraph (3) of this subsection;

(3) to immediately erect and maintain an enclosure for the potentially dangerous dog on the property where the potentially dangerous dog will be kept and maintained, which has sound sides, top and bottom to prevent the potentially dangerous dog from escaping by climbing, jumping or digging and within a fence of at least six feet in height separated by at least three feet from the confined area. The owner of a potentially dangerous dog shall securely lock the enclosure to prevent the entry of the general public and to preclude any release or escape of a potentially dangerous dog by an unknowing child or other person. All potentially dangerous dogs shall be confined in the enclosure or, if taken out of the enclosure, securely muzzled and restrained with a tether approved by the animal control officer and having a minimum tensile strength sufficiently in excess of that required to restrict the potentially dangerous dog's movements to a radius of no more than three feet from the owner and under the direct supervision of the owner;

b. may require the owner to comply with the following conditions:

(1) to maintain liability insurance in an amount determined by the panel to cover any damage or injury caused by the potentially dangerous dog. The liability insurance, which may be separate from any other homeowner policy, shall contain a provision requiring the municipality in which the owner resides to be named as an additional insured for the sole purpose of being notified by the insurance company of any cancellation, termination or expiration of the liability insurance policy;

(2) to tether the dog within the enclosure with a tether approved by the animal control officer and having a minimum tensile strength in excess of that required to fully secure the dog and of a length which prohibits the dog from climbing, jumping or digging out of the confined area.

L.1989, c. 307, § 8, eff. Jan. 12, 1990.

[1] Section 4:19–30.

4:19–25. Notice by official conducting panel hearing; compliance with uncontested finding; petition to municipal court; hearing de novo; findings; destruction or schedule for compliance

a. After the panel hearing, the official conducting the hearing shall notify in writing the owner of the dog, the animal control officer and the municipality in which the animal resides.

b. If the parties do not contest the panel's finding, the owner shall comply with the provisions of this act in accordance with a schedule established by the panel, but in no case more than 60 days subsequent to the date of determination.

c. If the panel's determination is contested, the contesting party may, within five days of such determination, bring a petition in the municipal court within the jurisdiction where the owner of the dog resides, requesting that the court conduct its own hearing on whether the dog should be declared vicious or potentially dangerous or whether the conditions imposed on the owner of a potentially dangerous dog are appropriate.

d. After service of the notice upon the parties to the action, the court shall conduct a hearing de novo and make its own determination.

e. If the court finds by a preponderance of the evidence that the dog is vicious, the dog shall be destroyed in a humane and expeditious manner, except that no dog may be destroyed during the pendency of an appeal.

f. If the court finds by a preponderance of the evidence that the dog is potentially dangerous, the court shall establish a schedule to insure compliance with this act, but in no case may complete compliance be allowed more than 60 days subsequent to the date of the court's determination.

g. If the dog has bitten or exposed a person within 10 days previous to the time of euthanasia, its head shall be transported to the New Jersey State Department of Health laboratory for rabies testing.

L.1989, c. 307, § 9, eff. Jan. 12, 1990.

4:19–26. Liability of owner for costs of impoundment and destruction

If a dog is declared vicious or potentially dangerous, and all appeals pertaining thereto have been exhausted, the owner of the dog shall be liable to the municipality in which the dog is impounded for the costs and expenses of impounding and destroying the dog. The municipality may establish by ordinance a schedule of these costs and expenses. The owner shall incur the expense of impounding the dog in a facility other than the municipal pound, regardless of whether the dog is ultimately found to be vicious or potentially dangerous.

L.1989, c. 307, § 10, eff. Jan. 12, 1990.

4:19–27. Right to convene hearing for subsequent actions of dog

If the municipal court or the panel finds that the dog is not vicious or potentially dangerous, the official responsible for convening a hearing pursuant to section 5 of this act [1] shall retain the right to convene a hearing to determine whether the dog is vicious or potentially dangerous for any subsequent actions of the dog.

L.1989, c. 307, § 11, eff. Jan. 12, 1990.

[1] Section 4:19–21.

4:19–28. Duties of owner of potentially dangerous dog

The owner of a potentially dangerous dog shall:

a. comply with the provisions of this act in accordance with a schedule established by the panel, but in no case more than 60 days subsequent to the date of determination;

b. notify the licensing authority, local police department or force, and the animal control officer if a potentially dangerous dog is at large, or has attacked a human being or killed a domestic animal;

c. notify the licensing authority, local police department or force, and the animal control officer within 24 hours of the death, sale or donation of a potentially dangerous dog;

d. prior to selling or donating the dog, inform the prospective owner that the dog has been declared potentially dangerous;

e. upon the sale or donation of the dog to a person residing in a different municipality, notify the department and the licensing authority, police department or force, and animal control officer of that municipality of the transfer of ownership and the name, address and telephone of the new owner; and

f. in addition to any license fee required pursuant to section 3 of P.L.1941, c. 151 (C.4:19-15.3), pay a potentially dangerous dog license fee to the municipality as provided by section 15 of this act.[1]

L.1989, c. 307, § 12, eff. Jan. 12, 1990.

1 Section 4:19–31.

4:19–29. Violations by owner; penalties; enforcement; seizure and impoundment of dog; destruction by order of court

The owner of a potentially dangerous dog who is found by a preponderance of the evidence to have violated this act, or any rule or regulation adopted pursuant thereto, or to have failed to comply with a panel's order shall be subject to a fine of not more than $1,000 per day of the violation, and each day's continuance of the violation shall constitute a separate and distinct violation. The municipal court shall have jurisdiction to enforce this section. An animal control officer is authorized to seize and impound any potentially dangerous dog whose owner fails to comply with the provisions of this act, or any rule or regulation adopted pursuant thereto, or a panel's order. The municipal court may order that the dog so seized and impounded be destroyed in an expeditious and humane manner.

L.1989, c. 307, § 13, eff. Jan. 12, 1990.

4:19–30. Potentially dangerous dog registration number, red identification tag and license; issuance; telephone number to report violations; publicity

Each municipality shall:

a. issue a potentially dangerous dog registration number and red identification tag along with a municipal potentially dangerous dog license upon a demonstration of sufficient evidence by the owner to the animal control officer that he has complied with the panel's orders. The last three digits of each potentially dangerous dog registration number issued by a municipality will be the three number code assigned to that municipality in the regulations promulgated pursuant to section 17 of this act.[1] The animal control officer shall verify, in writing, compliance to the municipal clerk or other official designated to license dogs in the municipality;

b. publicize a telephone number for reporting violations of this act. This telephone number shall be forwarded to the department and any changes in this number shall be reported immediately to the department.

L.1989, c. 307, § 14, eff. Jan. 12, 1990.

1 Section 4:19–33.

4:19–31. Fees for license

Every municipality may, by ordinance, fix the sum to be paid annually for a potentially dangerous dog license and each renewal thereof, which sum shall not be less than $150 nor more than $700. In the absence of any local ordinance, the fee for all potentially dangerous dog licenses shall be $150.

L.1989, c. 307, § 15, eff. Jan. 12, 1990.

4:19–32. Inspection to determine continuing compliance

The animal control officer shall inspect the enclosure and the owner's property at least monthly to determine continuing compliance with paragraphs (2) and (3) of subsection a. of section 8 of this act.[1]

L.1989, c. 307, § 16, eff. Jan. 12, 1990.

1 Section 4:19–24.

4:19–33. Regulations establishing uniform statewide system for municipal registration of potentially dangerous dogs

The department shall promulgate regulations establishing a uniform Statewide system for municipal registration of potentially dangerous dogs. The regulations shall assign each municipality or other authority registering potentially dangerous dogs a three number code. This three number code shall comprise the last three digits of each registration number issued by that municipality or authority for potentially dangerous dogs and shall be preceded on each dog's identification by a number sequentially issued by the municipality.

L.1989, c. 307, § 17, eff. Jan. 12, 1990.

4:19–34. Acts deemed exercise of government function; application of Tort Claims Act

Any action undertaken pursuant to the provisions of this act shall be deemed to be an exercise of a government function and shall be subject to the provisions of the "New Jersey Tort Claims Act," N.J.S.59:1–1 et seq.

L.1989, c. 307, § 18, eff. Jan. 12, 1990.

4:19–35. Deposit and use of fines and fees

All fines and fees collected or received by the municipality pursuant to sections 13 and 15 of this act[1] shall be deposited in a special account and used by the municipality to administer and enforce the provisions of this act.

L.1989, c. 307, § 20, eff. Jan. 12, 1990.

1 Sections 4:19–29 and 4:19–31.

4:19–36. Supersedure of local law, ordinance or regulation

The provisions of this act shall supersede any law, ordinance, or regulation concerning vicious or potentially dangerous dogs, any specific breed of dog, or any other type of dog inconsistent with this act enacted by any municipality, county, or county or local board of health.

L.1989, c. 307, § 21, eff. Jan. 12, 1990.

4:19–37. Inapplicability of act to dogs used for law enforcement activities

The provisions of this act shall not apply to dogs used for law enforcement activities.

L.1989, c. 307, § 22, eff. Jan. 12, 1990.

Discussion of New Jersey Vicious Dog Act

In his statement to the Senate, the governor quickly substantiates the need to exercise the state's preemption power. He notes a need for state-wide uniformity to deal with a "serious and widespread" threat that affects the "safety and welfare" of the citizens of the state. He further establishes the need for preemption in stating that local laws have proven inadequate.

As this is the governor's comment on a Senate bill that had been forwarded to him for his signature, he makes various recommendations for reconsideration and amendment. Note the fine hand of dog people in the language used—recognition that dog attacks are, in part, attributable to the failure of owners; prescribing the requirements for finding a dog "vicious" or "potentially dangerous"; the recognition of "qualified" individuals to sit on the panel of three. Finally the governor returns the enforcement of the provisions of the act to the municipal level. While the legislative portion has been preempted, few can object to the scheme, because they are still in charge of their own territory. This is politics at its finest.

Three aspects of this law are important: (1) preemption, (2) due process procedures and (3) criteria by which a dog is determined to be vicious or potentially dangerous.

Preemption: While this topic has been discussed theoretically in previous chapters, here consider the impact if it were not in place.

New Jersey is composed of a multitude of townships and cities, each of which constitutes a municipality. Some are large whereas others are small in both population and area. If each individual municipality had enacted a vicious dog ordinance, some breed-specific and others not, imagine a trip from one end of the state to the other with a dog that is or resembles some definition of a "pit bull." Starting from home, in a municipality that is presumed to have a generic ordinance, you drive three miles to another municipality, where your dog may be impounded because a police officer says it is a "pit bull." After dealing with the authorities, who determine that you do not have a "pit bull," you drive five more miles to another locality, where you are fined $500 because your "pit bull" is out in public without a muzzle. You may then proceed peacefully for about twenty more miles to another jurisdiction, where you are once again fined because you cannot show additional liability insurance for owning a "pit bull." An hour later you arrive within fifteen miles of your destination and your dog is shot and killed by a police officer because, he says, you have a "pit bull." Ludicrous? Yes. Possible? Perhaps. Desirable? Definitely not.

Preemption solves this problem. You may safely travel in New Jersey and some other states. However, not all have taken the step toward state-wide vicious dog legislation and we all take our chances when driving across state, county and municipal lines. For example, Dade County, Florida, has a breed-specific "pit bull" act that the Argentine Dogo may fall under. Miami, which is in Dade County, is a regular landing site for flights from South America. Two years ago I imported a top champion Dogo from Argentina. Friends checked with the authorities in Dade County and were told that the dog could land and be taken out of the county with no problem as long as the documentation was sufficient to establish his breed and that he was being removed from the county limits. Thus they arrived at the airport loaded with information and pictures, took possession of the dog in his crate, loaded him into their vehicle and headed for the Dade County border. Once they were across the county line, they stopped and exercised the dog. While it was unfair to the dog to have to remain in his crate and wait for an exercise break, it was for his own protection. Meanwhile, I was home wringing my hands until my friends called to say he was with them and out of Dade County. The dog is now in New Jersey, has a delightful, friendly, stable temperament typical of the breed and has been awarded numerous prizes in very strong competition.

Federal preemptive legislation is needed in this area, but will not come for some time. There must be a strong reason for the federal government to preempt the sovereign authority of the individual states. However, there are ways in which this could be accomplished. Remember that civil rights came under the Commerce Clause of the United States Constitution. However, as dogs are property and dog people have not been a vocal lot, it just hasn't attained the priority needed to force action.

The second important aspect of the New Jersey law is the due process requirement. The act provides for seizure and impoundment under specific circumstances. There is an option for the owner to have a say in where the dog is impounded. Then the procedure whereby a dog is determined to be vicious or potentially dangerous is laid out. The composition of the panel is detailed, notification requirements are specified, the conduct of the hearing is outlined but enough latitude is allowed for panel individuality, an evidentiary standard is set and the grounds for finding the dog vicious or potentially dangerous are defined. Finally, an appeal process is provided.

By providing an independent, quasi-legal/administrative type of process, all the parties to the incident will feel that they have some form of recourse. This alleviates the main danger of actions taken while tempers are high and fear is the controlling emotion.

In addition, the statute provides a scheme by which the owner can continue to maintain a dog that has been declared vicious or potentially dangerous. While this scheme is reminiscent of breed-specific legislation, it is only imposed after the initial panel has made its decision and all appeals from that ruling have been exhausted. At that point the decision to keep or dispose of the dog is the responsibility of the owner.

While any procedure in the hands of imperfect humans can fail or be abused, this scheme has proven to be equitable and effective in most situations.

Finally, I have included excerpts from the Dade County, Florida, and Denver, Colorado, breed-specific ordinances as a comparison.

PIT BULL ORDINANCE

(Dade County, Florida)

Sec. 5-17 Legislative Intent.

This article is intended to utilize the authority and powers of Metropolitan Dade County in order to secure for the citizens of this County the protection of their health, safety and welfare. It is intended to be applicable to dogs which are commonly referred to as "pit bulls" and which are defined herein. This article is designed to regulate these pit bull dogs and to ensure responsible handling by their owners through confinement, registration, and liability insurance. The pit bull dogs have been determined to require the special regulations and provisions contained within this article which the County Commission hereby finds reasonable and necessary.

Section 5-17.1. Definition and Identification of a Pit Bull Dog.

(a) The term "pit bull dog" as used within this article shall refer to any dog which exhibits those distinguishing characteristics which:

    (1) Substantially conform to the stadards established by the American Kennel Club for American Staffordshire Terriers or Staffordshire Bull Terriers; or

    (2) Substantially conform to the standards established by the United Kennel Club for American Pit Bull Terriers.

(b) The standards of the American Kennel Club and the United Kennel Club referred to in section (a) above, are attached hereto and incorporated herein by reference as "Exhibit A" and shall remain on file with the Animal Services Division of the Public Works Department of Metropolitan Dade County.

(c) Technical deficiencies in the dogs' conformance to the standards described in subsection (b) shall not be construed to indicate that the subject dog is not a "pit bull dog" under this article.

(d) Testimony by a veterinarian, zoologist, animal behaviorist, or animal control officer that a particular dog exhibits distinguishing physical characteristics of a pit bull shall establish a rebuttable presumption that the dog is a pit bull.

Sec. 5-17.2. Confinement of Pit Bull Dogs.

(a) Because of the pit bull dog's inbred propensity to attack other animals, and because of the danger posed to humans and animals alike by a pit bull dog when running loose or while running together in a pack, pit bull dogs must at all times be securely confined indoors, or confined in a securely and totally enclosed and locked pen, with either a top or with all four sides at least six (6) feet high, and with a conspicuous sign displaying the words "Dangerous Dog."

(b) At any time that a pit bull dog is not confined as required in subsection (a) above, the dog shall be muzzled in such a manner as to prevent it from biting or injuring any person or animal,

89

and kept on a leash with the owner or custodian in attendance. Provided, however, that no pit bull dog may be walked within fifty (50) feet of any public school ground nor enter onto such school ground.

(c) An exception to these confinement requirements is hereby provided for any pit bull dog in attendance at, and participating in, any lawful dog show, contest or exhibition sponsored by a dog club, association, society or similar organization.

(d) An exception to these confinement requirements is hereby provided for any pit bull dog when the dog is actually engaged in the sport of hunting in an authorized area and supervised by a competent person.

Sec. 5-17.3. Liability Insurance or Other Evidence of Financial Responsibility Required to be Maintained By Owner of Pit Bull Dogs.

In order to protect the public and to afford relief from the severe harm and injury which is likely to result from a pit bull dog attack, every owner of a pit bull dog shall maintain and be able to provide evidence of the owner's financial ability to respond in damages up to and including the amount of fifty thousand dollars ($50,000.00) for bodily injury to or death of any person or damage to property which may result from the ownership, keeping or maintenance of such dog. Proof of ability to respond in damages shall be given by filing with the animal control office a certificate of insurance from an insurance company authorized to do business in the state, stating that the owner is and will be insured against liability for such damages; or by posting with the animal control office a surety bond conditioned upon the payment of such damages during the period of such registration; or by posting a personal bond secured by a mortgage in real property or security interest in personal property; or a sworn statement of the owner of his/her financial ability to respond in damages up to an including the amount of fifty thousand dollars ($50,000.00).

Sec. 5-17.4. Registration of Pit Bull Dogs.

(a) Every owner of a pit bull dog in Metropolitan Dade County shall register the dog with the Animal Services Division of the Public Works Department of the County. The registration shall include the following: Name, address and telephone number of the dog's owner; the address where the dog is harbored, if different from the owner's address; a complete identification of the dog including the dog's sex, color and any other distinguishing physical characteristics; a color photograph of the dog; a description of the method of compliance with the confinement requirements; proof of the liability insurance or other evidence of financial responsibility required pursuant to this article; and a registration fee.

Sec. 5-17.5. Enforcement.

It shall be the duty and responsibility of all Metropolitan Dade County animal control officers to enforce the provisions of this article.

Sec. 5-17.6. Time for Compliance.

(a) All persons subject to this article shall have ninety (90) days from the effective date of this ordinance to comply with all confinement, registration, and liability insurance requirements.

(b) No pit bull dogs may be sold, purchased, obtained, brought into Dade County, or otherwise acquired by residents of Dade County anytime after the passage of ninety (90) days after the effective date of this ordinance. No such newly-acquired pit bull dogs may be kept, maintained, or otherwise harbored within Dade County, and each day any such newly-acquired pit bull is so kept, maintained, or harbored shall constitute a separate violation of this section.

No New Pit Bull Dogs After Aug. 14, 1989

    (1) Violation of subsection (b) may result in the issuance of a civil violation notice, and

    (2) Humane destruction of the pit bull dog by order of a court of competent jurisdiction. The County Manager or his designee may apply to the court for such order pursuant to this paragraph.

(c) Failure to register a pit bull dog as required by this article within the ninety (90) day grace period shall be prima facie evidence that the pit bull dog is a newly-acquired pit bull dog.

Sec. 8CC-10. Schedule of Civil Penalties.

Reference Number	Code Section	Description of Violation	Civil Penalty
*	*	* * * *	
7	5-8	Failure to obtain required license tag for dog	50.00
265	5-17.2	Failure to confine pit bull dog	500.00
266	5-17.3	Failure of owner of pit bull dog to maintain insurance or other evidence of financial responsibility	500.00
267	5-17.4	Failure to register pit bull dog	500.00
268	5-17.6	Acquisition or Keeping of Pit Bull dogs	500.00
*	*	* * *	

Section 11. If any section, subsection, sentence, clause or provision of this ordinance is held invalid, the remainder of this ordinance shall not be affected by such invalidity.

Section 12. Nothing in this article shall prevent municipalities from providing for more stringent regulation of pit bull dogs and pit bull dog owners.

Section 13. It is the intention of the Board of County Commissioners, and it is hereby ordained that the provisions of this ordinance shall become and be made a part of the Code of Metropolitan Dade County, Florida. The sections of this ordinance may be renumbered or relettered to accomplish such intention, and the word "ordinance" may be changed to "section," "article," or other appropriate word.

Section 14. This ordinance shall become effective ten (10) days after the date of enactment.

PIT BULL ORDINANCE
(Denver, Colorado)

Sec. 8-55. Pit bulls prohibited.

(a) It shall be unlawful for any person to own, possess, keep, exercise control over, maintain, harbor, transport, or sell within the city any pit bull.

(b) Definitions.

(1) An "owner," for purposes of this chapter, is defined as any person who owns, possesses, keeps, exercises control over, maintains, harbors, transports or sells an animal.

(2) A "pit bull," for purposes of this chapter, is defined as any dog that is an American Pit Bull Terrier, American Staffordshire Terrier, Staffordshire Bull Terrier, or any dog displaying the majority of physical traits of any one (1) or more of the above breeds, or any dog exhibiting those distinguishing characteristics which substantially conform to the standards established by the American Kennel Club or United Kennel Club for any of the above breeds. The A.K.C. and U.K.C. standards for the above breeds are on file in the office of the clerk and recorder, ex officio clerk of the City and County of Denver, at City Clerk Filing No. 89457.

(3) A "secure temporary enclosure," for purposes of this chapter, is a secure enclosure used for purposes of transporting a pit bull and which includes a top and bottom permanently attached to the sides except for a "door" for removal of the pit bull. Such enclosure must be of such material, and such door closed and secured in such a manner, that the pit bull cannot exit the enclosure on its own.

(c) Exceptions. The prohibition in subsection (a) of this section shall not apply in the following enumerated circumstances. Failure by the owner to comply and remain in compliance with all of the terms of any applicable exception shall subject the pit bull to immediate impoundment and disposal pursuant to subsection (e) of this section, and shall operate to prevent the owner from asserting such exception as a defense in any prosecution under subsection (a).

(1) The owner of a pit bull, who has applied for and received a dog license for such pit bull pursuant to section 8-61 at the Denver Municipal Animal Shelter on or before the date of publication of the ordinance enacting this section 8-55 [August 7, 1989], who has applied for and received a pit bull license in accordance with subsection (d) of this section, and who maintains the pit bull at all times in compliance with the put bull license requirements of subsection (d) of this section and all other applicable requirements of this chapter, may keep a pit bull within the city.

(2) The city's municipal animal shelter may

92

temporarily harbor and transport any pit bull for purposes of enforcing the provisions of this chapter.

(3) Any humane society operating an animal shelter which is registered and licensed by the city may temporarily hold any pit bull that it has received or otherwise recovered, but only for so long as it takes to contact the city's municipal animal shelter and either turn the pit bull over to the municipal animal shelter employees or receive permission to destroy or have destroyed the pit bull pursuant to the provisions of subsection (e).

(4) A person may temporarily transport into and hold in the city a pit bull only for the purpose of showing such pit bull in a place of public exhibition, contest or show sponsored by a dog club association or similar organization. However, the sponsor of the exhibition, contest, or show must receive written permission from the manager of health and hospitals, must obtain any other permits or licenses required by city ordinance, and must provide protective measures adequate to prevent pit bulls from escaping or injuring the public. The person who transports and holds a pit bull for showing shall, at all times when the pit bull is being transported within the city to and from the place of exhibition, contest, or show, keep the pit bull confined in a "secure temporary enclosure" as defined in subdivision (b)(3).

(5) Except as provided in subdivision (4), above, the owner of a pit bull may temporarily transport through the city a pit bull only if such owner has obtained a valid transport permit from the manager of health and hospitals. Upon request, the manager shall issue such permits only upon a showing by the owner that the pit bull is being transported either from a point outside the city to a destination outside the city, or from a point outside the city to an airport, train station or bus station within the city. In the latter case, such owner must provide evidence of an intent to send or take the pit bull outside of the city by producing an airline, train or bus ticket, or other equivalent document, showing a departure time within six (6) hours of the time of the transport. At all times when the pit bull is being transported within the city, it must be kept confined in a "secure temporary enclosure" as defined in subdivision (b)(3) of this section. In all cases before issuing a transport permit, the manager must find that the transport would not constitute an unnecessary or undue danger to the public health,

welfare or safety, and shall not issue the permit where the manager cannot so find. All transport permits issued shall only be valid for the time, date and pit bull specified on the permit, and shall not be construed to permit any activity otherwise prohibited.

(d) The owner of any pit bull which had been licensed pursuant to section 8-61 on or before the date of publication of the ordinance enacting this section 8-55 (Ordinance No. 404, Series of 1989) shall be allowed to keep such pit bull within the city upon compliance with the terms of the exception contained in subdivision (c)(1) of this section only if the owner applies for and receives an annual pit bull license on or before January 1, 1990. As a condition of issuance of a pit bull license, the owner shall at the time of application comply with or otherwise provide sufficient evidence that the owner is in compliance with *all* of the following regulations:

(1) The owner of the pit bull shall provide proof of rabies vaccination and shall pay the annual pit bull license fee of fifty dollars ($50.00).

(2) The owner of the pit bull shall keep current the license for such pit bull through annual renewal. Such license is not transferable and shall be renewable only by the holder of the license or by a member of the immediate family of such licensee. A pit bull license tag will be issued to the owner at the time of issuance of the license. Such license tag shall be attached to the pit bull by means of a collar or harness and shall not be attached to any pit bull other than the pit bull for which the license was issued. If the pit bull tag is lost or destroyed, a duplicate tag may be issued upon the payment of a two-dollar fee.

(3) The owner must be at least twenty-one (21) years of age as of January 1, 1990.

(4) The owner shall present to the manager proof that the owner has procured liability insurance in the amount of at least one hundred thousand dollars ($100,000.00), covering any damage or injury which may be caused by a pit bull during the twelve-month period covered by the pit bull license. The policy shall contain a provision requiring the insurance company to provide written notice to the manager not less than fifteen (15) days prior to any cancellation, termination, or expiration of the policy.

(5) The owner shall, at the owner's own expense, have the pit bull spayed or neutered and shall present to the manager documentary proof from a licensed veterinarian that this sterilization has been performed.

93

(6) The owner shall bring the pit bull to the Denver Municipal Animal Shelter where a person authorized by the manager shall cause a registration number assigned by the department to be tattooed or otherwise marked on the pit bull. The manager shall maintain a file containing the registration numbers and names of the pit bulls and the names and addresses of the owners. The owner shall notify the manager of any change of address.

(7) At all times when a pit bull is at the property of the owner, the owner shall keep the pit bull "confined," as that term is defined in subsection 8-52(b). At all times when a pit bull is away from the property of the owner, the owner shall keep the pit bull either securely leashed and muzzled or in a "secure temporary enclosure," as that term is defined in subdivision (b)(3) of this section.

(8) The owner shall not sell or otherwise transfer the pit bull to any person except a member of the owner's immediate family who will then become the owner and will be subject to all of the provisions of this section. The owner shall notify the manager within five (5) days in the event that the pit bull is lost, stolen, dies, or has a litter. In the event of a litter, the owner must deliver the puppies to the Denver Municipal Animal Shelter for destruction or permanently remove the puppies from Denver and provide sufficient evidence of such removal by the time the puppies are weaned, but in no event shall the owner be allowed to keep in Denver a pit bull puppy born after the date of publication of Ordinance No. 404, Series 1989, that is more than eight (8) weeks old. Any pit bull puppies kept contrary to the provisions of this subdivision are subject to immediate impoundment and disposal pursuant to subsection (e) of this section.

(9) The owner shall have posted at each possible entrance to the owner's property where the pit bull is kept a conspicuous and clearly legible pit bull sign. Such pit bull sign must be at least eight (8) inches by ten (10) inches in rectangular dimensions and shall contain only the words "PIT BULL DOG" in lettering not less than two (2) inches in height.

(e) Notwithstanding the provisions of Article VIII of this chapter, the manager of health and hospitals is authorized to immediately impound any pit bull found in the City and County of Denver which does not fall within the exceptions listed in subsection (c), above, and the municipal animal shelter may house or dispose of such pit bull in such manner as the manager may deem appropriate, except as the procedures in subsection (f), below, otherwise require.

(f) When the manager of health and hospitals has impounded any pit bull dog pursuant to this section, and the owner of such dog disputes the classification of such dog as a pit bull, the owner of such dog may file a written petition with the manager for a hearing concerning such classification no later than seven (7) days after impoundment. Such petition shall include the name and address, including mailing address, of the petitioner. The manager will then issue a notice of hearing date by mailing a copy to the petitioner's address no later than ten (10) days prior to the date of the hearing. Where no written request from the owner for a hearing is received by the manager within seven (7) days of impoundment, the pit bull shall be destroyed.

The hearing, if any, will be held before the manager or a hearing officer designated by the manager. Any facts which the petitioners wishes to be considered shall be submitted under oath or affirmation either in writing or orally at the hearing. The petitioner shall bear the risk of nonpersuasion. The manager or hearing officer shall make a final determination whether the dog is a pit bull as defined in subsection (b)(2) of this section. Such final determination shall be considered a final order of the manager subject to review under Rule 106(a)(4) of the state rules of civil procedure.

If the dog is found to be a pit bull, it shall be destroyed, unless the owner produces evidence deemed sufficient by the manager that the pit bull is to be permanently taken out of Denver and the owner pays the cost of impoundment. If the dog is found not to be a pit bull, the dog shall be released to the owner. The procedures in this subsection (f) shall not apply and the owner is not entitled to such a hearing with respect to any dog which was impounded as the immediate result of an attack or bite as defined in section 8-51. In those instances, the dog shall be handled and the procedures governed by the provisions of article VIII of this chapter.
(Ord. No. 404-89, § 1, 7-31-89; Ord. No. 631-89, § 1, 10-23-89)

Secs. 8-56—8-60. Reserved.

Much of the breed-specific or "pit bull" legislation relies on the United Kennel Club's American Pit Bull Terrier Standard and/or the American Kennel Club's American Staffordshire Terrier Standard. Then the ordinances state that any dog which substantially conforms to either standard is determined to be a "pit bull."

While there are problems with the standards, particularly the one used by the United Kennel Club, as it is brief, loosely structured and worded in broad terms, the real problem is who may determine if the dog exhibits distinguishing characteristics or substantially conforms to these standards.

Dade County, Florida, relies on the testimony of a veterinarian, zoologist, animal behaviorist or animal control officer. Many rely solely on their own law enforcement personnel, some of whom may be animal control officers, but not necessarily.

The real danger to our dogs depends on what action may be taken if a dog is "determined" to be a "pit bull." Some early laws authorized the immediate, on-site destruction of the animal. This is an outright violation of an individual's due process rights under the United States Constitution. Thus, most ordinances now call for impoundment of the dog until a hearing can be held. However, several problems arise from this action as well. If a dog is perceived by a law enforcement person as ready to attack, he may destroy the dog to protect himself and others. Also, while identification as a "pit bull" by a designated person as described by the statute is a rebuttable presumption, it is very difficult to prove otherwise since these laws are often couched in broad terms.

A number of breeds have been targeted by law enforcement and the general public as "pit bulls." These have been detailed in the following chart according to the characteristics contained in their respective breed Standards. As you can see, there are similarities normal to a "type" of breed as well as differences because they are different breeds. To the uninitiated, they may appear to be of the same breed unless all of them are lined up together. To the experienced person,

they are significantly different from each other. Note, however, that the United Kennel Club's American Pit Bull Terrier
and the American Kennel Club's American Staffordshire Terrier were the same breed in 1935. However, many breeders
within the two groups have since engaged in divergent breeding programs. While many may be dual-registered with the
two Kennel Clubs, there are differences.

Finally, the full Standard for each breed detailed in the
chart has been provided for further study. However, remember that there are other breeds that can fall into this broad
category as well as a number of other breeds that may be
targeted in the future.

	AMERICAN PIT BULL TERRIER	AMERICAN STAFFORDSHIRE TERRIER
GROUP	Terrier	Terrier
SIZE	N/A	M: 18"–19" F: 17"–18"
Weight	M: 35–60 lbs. F: 30–50 lbs.	In proportion to height
GENERAL APPEARANCE	Muscular	Muscular/stocky
HEAD	Bricklike	Medium length Broad skull
EARS	Cropping optional	Cropped preferred Uncropped allowed
EYES	Round Any color	Round Dark
NOSE	Open nostrils Any color	Black
LIPS	Any color	Close and even
BITE	Scissors	Scissors
NECK	Muscular Slightly arched	Heavy Slightly arched

SHOULDERS	Strong and muscular	Strong and muscular
CHEST	Deep	Deep and broad
BACK	Short and strong	Fairly short
TOPLINE	Slightly sloping	Slightly sloping
REAR	Well muscled	Well muscled
TAIL	Short, low-set Tapering	Short, low-set Tapering
COAT	Short and stiff	Short and stiff
COLOR	Any color or marking	Any color, solid, parti, patched permissible: All white, more than 80% White, black and tan, and liver not encouraged
CHARACTER	N/A	Keenly alive to surroundings

	ARGENTINE DOGO	BOXER
GROUP	Working	Working
SIZE	M: Minimum 24½″ F: Minimum 23½″ 27″ suggested maximum	M: 22½″–25″ F: 21″–23½″
WEIGHT	80–100 lbs.	N/A
GENERAL APPEARANCE	Muscular and athletic	Good substance, agile
HEAD	Skull broad, convex/concave structure	Clean/harmonious proportions
EARS	Cropped short	Cropped long
EYES	Wide-set, intense Hazel to dark brown	Dark brown

	ARGENTINE DOGO	BOXER
NOSE	Well-developed nostrils Black	Broad Black
LIPS	Close-fitting, black	Thick, padded upper lip
BITE	Scissors	Undershot
NECK	Thick, softly arched	Round, muscular, elegant arch
SHOULDERS	High, strongly muscled	Long, sloping
CHEST	Wide and deep	Fairly wide, well-defined forechest
BACK	Higher at the withers	Smooth, firm
TOPLINE	Softly sloping to rump	Slightly sloping
REAR	Muscular thighs	Strongly muscled, thighs broad and curved
TAIL	Long and thick	Docked, set high
COAT	Short	Short and smooth
COLOR	White	Fawn or brindle
CHARACTER	Stable and self-assured	Alert, dignified and self-assured

	BULLDOG	CHINESE SHAR-PEI
GROUP	Non-sporting	Non-sporting
SIZE	Medium-sized	18"–20"
WEIGHT	M: 50 lbs. F: 40 lbs.	40–55 lbs.
GENERAL APPEARANCE	Heavy, thickset low-slung body	Close-coupled, square profile
HEAD	Very large	Large, wrinkled

EARS	Rose-eared	Small, triangular, lie flat against head pointing toward eyes
EYES	Round, low-set, dark	Small, almond and sunken Dark
NOSE	Large, broad and black	Large, wide, darkly pigmented (some self-colored—dilutes)
LIPS	Thick, pendant flews	Well padded, bluish-black tongue
BITE	Undershot	Scissors
NECK	Short, thick and well-arched	Medium length, moderate to heavy folds of skin
SHOULDERS	Widespread, slanting outward	Muscular, well laid back, Sloping
CHEST	Broad, deep, full	Broad and deep
BACK	Short, strong, broad at shoulders, narrow at loins	Short, close-coupled
TOPLINE	Roach-back/wheel-back	Slight dip behind withers, slight rise over loin
REAR	Muscular, longer than forelegs, feet point out	Muscular, moderately angulated
TAIL	Short, hung low: Straight or screwed	Thick tapering to a fine point, set high, curls over or to either side of back
COAT	Straight, short, flat	Harsh—short horse coat or longer brush coat

	BULLDOG	CHINESE SHAR-PEI
COLOR	Pure, uniform, brilliant brindle, solid white, red, fawn or fallow, piebald	Solid colors only with/without shading
CHARACTER	Dignified, pacific, yet courageous	Regal, alert, standoffish

BULL TERRIER

GROUP	Terrier
SIZE	N/A
WEIGHT	N/A
GENERAL APPEARANCE	Muscular, symmetrical, active
HEAD	Long, strong and deep
EARS	Small, thin, erect
EYES	Well sunken, dark
NOSE	Well-developed nostrils, black
LIPS	Clean and tight
BITE	Level or scissors
NECK	Cleanly muscled, long and arched
SHOULDERS	Strong and muscular
CHEST	Broad
BACK	Short and strong
TOPLINE	Slightly arched over the loin
REAR	Muscular thighs
TAIL	Short and fine, set low
COAT	Short, flat, harsh and glossy
COLOR	White with head markings allowed or any color other than white or any color with white markings
CHARACTER	Amenable, sweet, yet full of fire

OFFICIAL STANDARD FOR THE AMERICAN PIT BULL TERRIER

Head—Medium length. Bricklike in shape. Skull flat and widest at the ears, with prominent cheeks free from wrinkles.

Muzzle—Square, wide and deep. Well-pronounced jaws, displaying strength. Upper teeth should meet tightly over lower teeth, outside in front.

Ears—Cropped or uncropped (not important). Should set high on head, and be free from wrinkles.

Eyes—Round. Should be set far apart, low down on skull. Any color acceptable.

Nose—Wide-open nostrils. Any color acceptable.

Neck—Muscular. Slightly arched. Tapering from shoulder to head. Free from looseness of skin.

Shoulders—Strong and muscular, with wide sloping shoulder blades.

Back—Short and strong. Slightly sloping from withers to rump. Slightly arched at loins, which should be slightly tucked.

Chest—Deep, but not too broad, with wide sprung ribs.

Ribs—Close. Well sprung, with deep back ribs.

Tail—Short in comparison to size. Set low and tapering to a fine point. Not carried over back. Bobbed tail not acceptable.

Legs—Large, round-boned, with straight, upright pasterns, reasonably strong. Feet to be of medium size. Gait should be light and springy. No rolling or pacing.

Thigh—Long with muscles developed. Hocks down and straight.

Coat—Short and stiff to the touch.

Color—Any color or marking permissible.

Weight—Not important. Females preferred from 30 to 50 pounds. Males from 35 to 60 pounds.

Scale of Points:

General appearance, personality, obedience	20
Head, muzzle, eye, ears	25
Neck, shoulder, and chest	15
Body	15
Legs and feet	15
Tail, coat and color	10
Total	100

United Kennel Club Standard, January 1, 1978

OFFICIAL STANDARD FOR THE AMERICAN STAFFORDSHIRE TERRIER

General Appearance—The American Staffordshire Terrier should give the impression of great strength for his size, a well-put-together dog, muscular, but agile and graceful, keenly alive to his surroundings. He should be stocky, not long-legged or racy in outline. His courage is proverbial.

Head—Medium length, deep through, broad skull, very pronounced cheek muscles, distinct stop; and ears are set high.

Ears—Cropped or uncropped, the latter preferred. Uncropped ears should be short and held half rose or prick. Full drop to be penalized.

Eyes—Dark and round, low down in skull and set far apart. No pink eyelids.

Muzzle—Medium length, rounded on upper side to fall away abruptly below eyes. Jaws well defined. Underjaw to be strong and have biting power. Lips close and even, no looseness. Upper teeth to meet tightly outside lower teeth in front. Nose definitely black.

Neck—Heavy, slightly arched, tapering from shoulders to back of skull. No looseness of skin. Medium length.

Shoulders—Strong and muscular with blades wide and sloping.

Many people consider the American Staffordshire Terrier or any other dog resembling it to be a "pit bull". The term is actually generic. What is recognized by AKC as an American Staffordshire Terrier is, with very little or no difference, recognized by UKC as an American Pit Bull Terrier. Cross-breeding with other kinds of dogs has confused identity even further.

Argentine Dogo Club of America Ch. Ganymede Stormy Weather, owned by Deidre E. Gannon and Linda Smith, is a typical example of this interesting guard dog/hunting breed developed in Argentina during the twentieth century. *Bruce Harkins*

Back—Fairly short. Slight sloping from withers to rump with gentle short slope at rump to base of tail. Loins slightly tucked.
Body—Well-sprung ribs, deep in rear. All ribs close together. Forelegs set rather wide apart to permit chest development. Chest deep and broad.
Tail—Short in comparison to size, low-set, tapering to a fine point; not curled or held over back. Not docked.
Legs—The front legs should be straight, large or round bones, pastern upright. No resemblance of bend in front. Hindquarters well muscled, let down at hocks, turning neither in nor out. Feet of moderate size, well arched and compact. Gait must be springy but without roll or pace.
Coat—Short, close, stiff to the touch, and glossy.
Color—Any color, solid, parti or patched is permissible, but all white, more than 80 percent white, black and tan, and liver not to be encouraged.
Size—Height and weight should be in proportion. A height of about 18 to 19 inches at shoulders for the male and 17 to 18 inches for the female is to be considered preferable.
Faults—Faults to be penalized are: Dudley nose, light or pink eyes, tail too long or badly carried, undershot or overshot mouth.

Approved June 10, 1936

ARGENTINE DOGO
OFFICIAL STANDARD REVISION

General Appearance—The Argentine Dogo is a finely developed athlete. He should possess a perfectly proportioned and balanced structure. The Musculature is well developed denoting power and strength. His free and easy movement displays agility and indicates endurance. He has a high energy level with an alert, intense and intelligent expression. The short, white coat serves to accentuate his overall muscular harmony. As a working dog, he participates in every activity from start to finish. Thus, in judging the breed the Dogo should be evaluated as a whole dog with no emphasis given to any one part.

Height—Adult males 24½ to 26½ inches; adult females 23½ to 25½ inches at the withers. An inch or more over the maximum preferred range is acceptable provided that balance and proportion are maintained. Adults under minimum height must be disqualified.

Weight—In proportion to height. Average: 88–100 lbs.

Head and Muzzle—The skull is broad with well-developed cheeks tapering slightly into the muzzle. The skull and the muzzle should be of equal length. Seen from the side the top of the skull is slightly rounded. The top of the muzzle is straight with an upward tilt at the nose so that the nose is slightly higher than the stop.

Eyes—Hazel to dark brown. Eye rims may be flesh colored or black edged. Eyes should be wide set.

Expression—Alert, intense and intelligent.

Ears—Cropped short and triangular in shape. Well set at the top of the head.

Nose—Black with well-developed nostrils. The nose is neither pointed nor square, but slightly blunted at the end.

Jaws and Bite—Jaws must be well developed with large, healthy teeth. Scissors bite is preferred; level bite is acceptable. A reverse scissors bite should be faulted. Overshot or undershot jaws must be disqualified. Full dentition is preferred but the absence of one or more pre-molars is not to be faulted.

Lips—Close fitting with black pigmentation. The corners of the lips may protrude slightly but must not have any suggestion of looseness or dewlap.

Neck—The neck is thick with a gentle arch. The skin is thick with some wrinkling in the throat region.

Topline—Strong and firm with a slight rise over the loin. It should remain firm and flat when the dog is moving.

Chest—The chest is broad and deep with well-sprung ribs. When viewed from the front or side the chest should reach just below the elbows.

Body—Slightly off square. The ratio of height to length is as 9 is to 10. The body is solid with good bone and an athletically developed musculature.

Shoulders—Strongly developed and well laid back at or approaching a 45° angle.

Forequarters—Straight and strong with good bone. Pasterns will slope slightly from the perpendicular for functional purposes. Front dewclaws may be removed.

Hindquarters—Moderately angulated with strong, muscular thighs and well let down hocks. Rear dewclaws must be removed.

Feet—Compact with tight, well-arched toes. Thick, rough and well-cushioned pads.

Tail—Long, thick and tapering to a point. Just reaching the hock when hanging naturally at rest. When excited the dog carries it high and moving from side to side. It should never curl over the back.

Coat—Short, flat and close to the body. Slightly coarse to the touch.

Skin—Due to the nature of the close, single coat even the slightest skin abrasion, resulting from work or play, will show and should not be penalized.

Color—White. Skin pigmentation may show through the coat, but should not be excessive. One patch on the head or minor coat ticking is acceptable.

Gait—Free and easy movement combine agility, strength and endurance.

Character and Temperament—Stable and courageous. Steady in all circumstances.

Disqualifications

Blue eyes.
Bi-lateral deafness.
Undershot or overshot jaws.
Adult under minimum height.

Argentine Dogo Club of America, Inc.
October 1993

The **Boxer** is one of our most familiar, best-loved dog breeds. Developed in Germany, his original name, "Bullenbeiser" or "Bull Biter," tells us that he was used at one time to control and subdue livestock.

The **Bull Terrier** is often thought of by the casual observer as a "pit bull." This breed was in fact used as a fighting dog in England prior to the ban on blood sports there. Today's Bull Terrier, while as self-sufficient and courageous as his ancestors, is thought by many as the ideal companion.

OFFICIAL STANDARD FOR THE BOXER

General Appearance—The *ideal* Boxer is a medium-sized, square-built dog of good substance with short back, strong limbs, and short, tight-fitting coat. His well-developed muscles are clean, hard and appear smooth under taut skin. His movements denote energy. The gait is firm, yet elastic, the stride free and ground-covering, the carriage proud. Developed to serve as guard, working and companion dog, he combines strength and agility with elegance and style. His expression is alert and temperament steadfast and tractable.

The chiseled head imparts to the Boxer a unique individual stamp. It must be in correct proportion to the body. The broad, blunt muzzle is the distinctive feature, and great value is placed upon its being of proper form and balance with the skull.

In judging the Boxer, first consideration is given to general appearance, to which attractive color and arresting style contribute. Next is overall balance with special attention devoted to the head, after which the individual body components are examined for their correct construction, and efficiency of gait is evaluated.

Size, Proportion, Substance, Height—Adult males 22½ to 25 inches; females 21 to 23½ inches at the withers. Preferably, males should not be under the minimum nor females over the maximum; however, proper balance and quality in the individual should be of primary importance since there is no size disqualification. *Proportion*—The body in profile is of square proportion in that a horizontal line from the front of the forechest to the rear projection of the upper thigh should equal the length of a vertical line dropped from the top of the withers to the ground. *Substance*—Sturdy with balanced musculature. Males larger-boned than their female counterparts.

Head—The beauty of the head depends upon harmonious proportion of muzzle to skull. The blunt muzzle is one-third the length of the head from the occiput to the tip of the nose, and two-thirds the width of the skull. The head should be clean, not showing deep wrinkles (wet). Wrinkles typically appear upon the forehead when ears are erect, and folds are always present from the lower edge of the stop running downward on both sides of the muzzle. *Expression*—Intelligent and alert. *Eyes*—Dark brown in color, not too small, too protruding or too deep-set. Their mood-mirroring character, combined with the wrinkling of the forehead, gives the Boxer head its unique quality of expressiveness. *Ears*—Set at the highest points of the sides of the skull are cropped, cut rather long and tapering, raised when alert. *Skull*—The top of the skull is slightly arched, not rounded, flat or noticeably broad, with the occiput not overly pronounced. The forehead shows a slight indentation between the eyes and forms a distinct stop with the topline of the muzzle. The cheeks should be relatively flat and not bulge (cheekiness), maintaining the clean lines of the skull, and should taper into the muzzle in a slight, graceful curve. *Muzzle*—The muzzle, proportionately developed in length, width and depth, has a shape influenced first through the formation of both jawbones, second through the placement of the teeth, and third through the texture of the lips. The top of the muzzle should not slant down (down-faced), nor should it be concave (dish-faced); however, the tip of the nose should lie slightly higher than the root of the muzzle.

The nose should be broad and black.

The upper jaw is broad where attached to the skull and maintains this breadth except for a very slight tapering to the front. The lips, which complete the formation of the muzzle, should meet evenly in front. The upper lip is thick and padded, filling out the frontal space created by the projection of the lower jaw, and laterally is supported by the canines of the lower jaw. Therefore, these canines must stand far apart and be of good length so that the front surface of the muzzle is broad and squarish and, when viewed from the side, shows moderate layback. The chin should be perceptible from the side as well as from the front. *Bite*—The Boxer bite is undershot; the lower jaw protrudes beyond the upper and curves slightly upward. The incisor teeth of the lower jaw are in a straight line, with the canines preferably up front in the same line to give the jaw the greatest possible width. The upper line of incisors is slightly convex with the corner upper incisors fitting snugly back of the lower canine teeth on each side. *Faults*—Skull too broad. Cheekiness. Wrinkling too deep (wet) or lacking (dry). Excessive flews. Muzzle too light for skull. Too pointed a bite (snipy), too undershot, teeth or tongue showing when mouth closed. Eyes noticeably lighter than ground color of coat.

Neck, Topline, Body—*Neck*—Round, of ample length, muscular and clean without excessive hanging skin (dewlap). The neck has a distinctly marked nape with an elegant arch blending smoothly into the withers. *Topline*—Smooth, firm and slightly sloping.

Body—The chest is of fair width, and the forechest well defined and visible from the side. The brisket is deep, reaching down to the elbows; the depth of the body at the lowest point of the brisket equals half the height of the dog at the withers. The ribs, extending far to the rear, are well arched but not barrel-shaped. The back is short, straight and muscular and firmly connects the withers to the hindquarters. The loins are short and muscular. The lower stomach line is slightly tucked up, blending into a graceful curve to the rear. The croup is slightly sloped, flat and broad. Tail is set high, docked and carried upward. Pelvis long and in females especially broad. *Faults*—Short heavy neck. Chest too broad, too narrow or hanging between shoulders. Lack of forechest. Hanging stomach. Slab-sided rib cage. Long or narrow loin, weak union with croup. Falling off of croup. Higher in rear than in front.

Forequarters—The shoulders are long and sloping, close-lying, and not excessively covered with muscle (loaded). The upper arm is long, approaching a right angle to the shoulder blade. The elbows should not press too closely to the chest wall nor stand off visibly from it. The forelegs are long, straight and firmly muscled and when viewed from the front, stand parallel to each other. The pastern is strong and distinct, slightly slanting, but standing almost perpendicular to the ground. The dewclaws may be removed. Feet should be compact, turning neither in nor out, with well-arched toes. *Faults*—Loose or loaded shoulders. Tied-in or bowed-out elbows.

Hindquarters—The hindquarters are strongly muscled with angulation in balance with that of the forequarters. The thighs are broad and curved, the breech musculature hard and strongly developed. Upper and lower thigh long. Leg well angulated at the stifle with a clearly defined, well "let down" hock joint. Viewed from behind, the hind legs should be straight with hock joints leaning neither in nor out. From the side, the leg below the hock (metatarsus) should be almost perpendicular to the ground, with a slight slope to the rear permissible. The metatarsus should be short, clean and strong. The Boxer has no rear dewclaws. *Faults*—Steep or over-angulated hindquarters. Light thighs or overdeveloped hams. Over-angulated (sickle) hocks. Hindquarters too far under or too far behind.

Coat—Short, shiny, lying smooth and tight to the body.

Color—The colors are fawn and brindle. Fawn shades vary from light tan to mahogany. The brindle ranges from sparse, but clearly defined black stripes on a fawn background, to such a heavy concentration of black striping that the essential fawn background color barely, although clearly, shows through (which may create the appearance of "reverse brindling"). White markings should be of such distribution as to enhance the dog's appearance, but may not exceed one-third of the entire coat. They are not desirable on the flanks or on the back of the torso proper. On the face, white may replace part of the otherwise essential black mask and may extend in an upward path between the eyes, but it must not be excessive, so as to detract from true Boxer expression. *Faults*—Unattractive or misplaced white markings. *Disqualifications*—

Boxers that are any color other than fawn or brindle. Boxers with a total of white markings exceeding one-third of the entire coat.

Gait—Viewed from the side, proper front and rear angulation is manifested in a smoothly efficient, level-backed, ground-covering stride with powerful drive emanating from a freely operating rear. Although the front legs do not contribute impelling power, adequate "reach" should be evident to prevent interference, overlap or "sidewinding" (crabbing). Viewed from the front, the shoulders should remain trim and the elbows not flare out. The legs are parallel until gaiting narrows the track in proportion to increasing speed, then the legs come in under the body but should never cross. The line from the shoulder down through the leg should remain straight although not necessarily perpendicular to the ground. Viewed from the rear, a Boxer's rump should not roll. The hind feet should "dig in" and track relatively true with the front. Again, as speed increases, the normally broad rear track will become narrower. *Faults*—Stilted or inefficient gait. Lack of smoothness.

Character and Temperament—These are of paramount importance in the Boxer. Instinctively a "hearing" guard dog, his bearing is alert, dignified and self-assured. In the show ring, his behavior should exhibit constrained animation. With family and friends, his temperament is fundamentally playful, yet patient and stoical with children. Deliberate and wary with strangers, he will exhibit curiosity but, most importantly, fearless courage if threatened. However, he responds promptly to friendly overtures honestly rendered. His intelligence, loyal affection and tractability to discipline make him a highly desirable companion. *Faults*—Lack of dignity and alertness. Shyness.

Disqualifications

Boxers that are any color other than fawn or brindle. Boxers with a total of white markings exceeding one-third of the entire coat.

Approved March 14, 1989

OFFICIAL STANDARD FOR THE BULL TERRIER

White

The Bull Terrier must be strongly built, muscular, symmetrical and active, with a keen, determined and intelligent expression, full of fire but of sweet disposition and amenable to discipline.

Head—Should be long, strong and deep right to the end of the muzzle, but not coarse. Full face it should be oval in outline and be filled completely up, giving the impression of fullness with a surface devoid of hollows or indentations, i.e., egg-shaped. In profile it should curve gently downward from the top of the skull to the tip of the nose. The forehead should be flat across from ear to ear. The distance from the tip of the nose to the eyes should be perceptibly greater than that from the eyes to the top of the skull. The underjaw should be deep and well defined. The *Lips* should be clean and tight. The *Teeth* should meet in either a level or in a scissors bite. In the scissors bite the upper teeth should fit in front of and closely against the lower teeth, and they should be sound, strong and perfectly regular. The *Ears* should be small, thin and placed close together. They should be capable of being held stiffly erect, when they should point upward. The *Eyes* should be well sunken and as dark as possible, with a piercing glint, and they should be small, triangular and obliquely placed; set near together and high up on the dog's head. Blue eyes are a disqualification. The *Nose* should be black, with well-developed nostrils bent downward at the tip. **Neck**—Should be very muscular, long, arched and clean, tapering from the shoulders to the head and it should be free from loose skin. The *Chest* should be broad when viewed from in front, and there should be great depth from withers to brisket, so that the latter is nearer the ground than the belly. **Body**—Should be well rounded with marked spring of rib, the back should be short and strong. The back ribs deep. Slightly arched over the loin. The shoulders should be strong and muscular but without heaviness. The shoulder blades should be wide and flat and there should be a very pronounced backward slope from the bottom edge of the blade to the top edge. Behind the shoulders there should be no slackness or dip at the withers. The underline from the brisket to the belly should form a graceful upward curve.

Legs—Should be big-boned but not to the point of coarseness; the forelegs should be of moderate length, perfectly straight, and the dog must stand firmly upon them. The elbows must turn neither in nor out, and the pasterns should be strong and upright. The hind legs should be parallel viewed from behind. The thighs very muscular with hocks well let down. Hind pasterns short and upright. The stifle joint should be well bent with a well-developed second thigh. The *Feet* round and compact with well-arched toes like a cat.

Tail—Should be short, set on low, fine, and ideally should be carried horizontally. It should be thick where it joins the body, and should taper to a fine point.

Coat—Should be short, flat, harsh to the touch and with a fine gloss. The dog's skin should fit tightly. The *Color* is white though markings on the head are permissible. Any markings elsewhere on the coat are to be severely faulted. Skin pigmentation is not to be penalized.

Movement—The dog shall move smoothly, covering the ground with free, easy strides, forelegs and hind legs should move parallel each to each when viewed from in front or behind. The forelegs reaching out well and hind legs moving smoothly at the hip and flexing well at the stifle and hock.

The dog should move compactly and in one piece but with a typical jaunty air that suggests agility and power.

Faults

Any departure from the foregoing points shall be considered a fault, and the seriousness of the fault shall be in exact proportion to its degree, i.e., a very crooked front is a very bad fault; a rather crooked front is a rather bad fault; and a slightly crooked front is a slight fault.

Disqualification

Blue eyes.

Colored

The Standard for the Colored Variety is the same as for the White except for the subhead "Color" which reads: *Color.* Any color other than white, or any color with white markings. Other things being equal, the preferred color is brindle. A dog which is predominantly white shall be disqualified.

Disqualifications

Blue eyes.
Any dog which is predominantly white.

Approved July 9, 1974

OFFICIAL STANDARD FOR THE BULLDOG

General Appearance—The perfect Bulldog must be of medium size and smooth coat; with heavy, thickset, low-swung body, massive short-faced head, wide shoulders and sturdy limbs. The general appearance and attitude should suggest great stability, vigor and strength. The disposition should be equable and kind, resolute and courageous (not vicious or aggressive), and demeanor should be pacific and dignified. These attributes should be countenanced by the expression and behavior.

Size, Proportion, Symmetry—*Size*—The size for mature dogs is about 50 pounds; for mature bitches about 40 pounds. *Proportion*—The circumference of the skull in front of the ears should measure at least the height of the dog at the shoulders. *Symmetry*—The "points" should be well distributed and bear good relation one to the other, no feature being in such prominence from either excess or lack of quality that the animal appears deformed or ill-proportioned. *Influence of Sex*—In comparison of specimens of different sex, due allowance should be made in favor of the bitches, which do not bear the characteristics of the breed to the same degree of perfection and grandeur as do the dogs.

Head—Eyes and Eyelids—The eyes, seen from the front, should be situated low down in the skull, as far from the ears as possible, and their corners should be in a straight line at right angles with the stop. They should be quite in front of the head, as wide apart as possible, provided their outer corners are within the outline of the cheeks when viewed from the front. They should be quite round in form, of moderate size, neither sunken nor bulging, and in color should be very dark. The lids should cover the white of the eyeball when the dog is looking directly forward, and the lid should show no "haw." *Ears*—The ears should be set high in the head, the front inner edge of each ear joining the outline of the skull at the top back corner of skull, so as to place them as wide apart, and as high, and as far from the eyes as possible. In size they should be small and thin. The shape termed "rose ear" is the most desirable. The rose ear folds inward at its back lower edge, the upper front edge curving over, outward and backward, showing part of the inside of the burr. (The ears should not be carried erect or prick-eared or buttoned and should never be cropped.) *Skull*—The skull should be very large, and in circumference, in front of the ears, should measure at least the height of the dog at the shoulders. Viewed from the front, it should appear very high from the corner of the lower jaw to the apex of the skull, and also very broad and square. Viewed at the side, the head should appear very high, and very short from the point of the nose to occiput. The forehead should be flat (not rounded or domed), neither too prominent nor overhanging the face. *Cheeks*—The cheeks should be well rounded, protruding sideways and outward beyond the eyes. *Stop*—The temples or frontal bones should be very well defined, broad, square and high, causing a hollow or groove between the eyes. This indentation, or stop, should be both broad and deep and extend up the middle of the forehead, dividing the head vertically, being traceable to the top of the skull. *Face and Muzzle*—The face, measured from the front of the cheekbone to the tip of the nose, should be extremely short, the muzzle being very short, broad, turned upward and very deep from the corner of the eye to the corner of the mouth. *Nose*—The nose should be large, broad and black, its tip set back deeply between the eyes. The distance from bottom of stop, between the eyes, to the tip of nose should be as short as possible and not exceed the length from the tip of nose to the edge of underlip. The nostrils should be wide, large and black, with a well-defined line between them. Any nose other than black is objectionable and a brown or liver-colored nose shall *disqualify*. *Lips*—The chops or "flews" should be thick, broad, pendant and very deep, completely overhanging the lower jaw at each side. They join the underlip in front and almost or quite cover the teeth, which should be scarcely noticeable when the mouth is closed. *Bite—Jaws*—The jaws should be massive, very broad, square and "undershot," the lower jaw projecting considerably in front of the upper jaw and turning up. *Teeth*—The teeth should be large and strong, with the canine teeth or tusks wide apart, and the six small teeth in front, between the canines, in an even, level row.

Neck, Topline, Body—*Neck*—The neck should be short, very

thick, deep and strong and well arched at the back. *Topline*—
There should be a slight fall in the back, close behind the
shoulders (its lowest part), whence the spine should rise to
the loins (the top of which should be higher than the top of
the shoulders), thence curving again more suddenly to the
tail, forming an arch (a very distinctive feature of the breed),
termed "roach-back" or, more correctly, "wheel-back." *Body*—
The brisket and body should be very capacious, with full
sides, well-rounded ribs and very deep from the shoulders
down to its lowest part, where it joins the chest. It should be
well let down between the shoulders and forelegs, giving the
dog a broad, low, short-legged appearance. *Chest*—The chest
should be very broad, deep and full. *Underline*—The body
should be well ribbed up behind with the belly tucked up and
not rotund. *Back and Loin*—The back should be short and
strong, very broad at the shoulders and comparatively narrow
at the loins. *Tail*—The tail may be either straight or "screwed"
(but never curved or curly), and in any case must be short,
hung low, with decided downward carriage, thick root and
fine tip. If straight, the tail should be cylindrical and of uniform taper. If "screwed," the bends or kinks should be well
defined, and they may be abrupt and even knotty, but no portion of the member should be elevated above the base or root.
Forequarters—*Shoulders*—The shoulders should be muscular, very heavy, widespread and slanting outward, giving stability and great power. *Forelegs*—The forelegs should be
short, very stout, straight and muscular, set wide apart, with
well developed calves, presenting a bowed outline, but the
bones of the legs should not be curved or bandy, nor the feet
brought too close together. *Elbows*—The elbows should be low
and stand well out and loose from the body. *Feet*—The feet
should be moderate in size, compact and firmly set. Toes compact, well split up, with high knuckles and very short stubby
nails. The front feet may be straight or slightly out-turned.
Hindquarters—*Legs*—The hind legs should be strong and
muscular and longer than the forelegs, so as to elevate the
loins above the shoulders. Hocks should be slightly bent and

The universally-renowned Bulldog is synonymous with courage and determination. Today's version is much different from the original that was used in bullbaiting and other gruesome blood sports once legal in England.

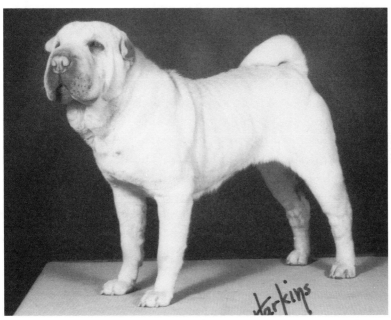

The Chinese Shar-Pei is truly a modern phenomenon in the world of dogs. Virtually unknown outside its homeland prior to the late 1960s, this unusual breed has experienced a groundswell of popularity and is today a solid success story. This is in sharp contrast to the brush this ancient fighting dog had with extinction at the hands of the Communist Chinese. The model is Ming Yu Dairy Queen, owned by Linda Teitelbaum. *Bruce Harkins*

119

well let down, so as to give length and strength from the loins to hock. The lower leg should be short, straight and strong, with the stifles turned slightly outward and away from the body. The hocks are thereby made to approach each other, and the hind feet to turn outward. *Feet*—the feet should be moderate in size, compact and firmly set. Toes compact, well split up, with high knuckles and short stubby nails. The hind feet should be pointed well outward.

Coat and Skin—*Coat*—The coat should be straight, short, flat, close, of fine texture, smooth and glossy. (No fringe, feather or curl.) *Skin*—The skin should be soft and loose, especially at the head, neck and shoulders. *Wrinkles and Dewlap*—The head and face should be covered with heavy wrinkles, and at the throat, from jaw to chest, there should be two loose pendulous folds, forming the dewlap.

Color of Coat—The color of coat should be uniform, pure of its kind and brilliant. The various colors found in the breed are to be preferred in the following order: (1) red brindle, (2) all other brindles, (3) solid white, (4) solid red, fawn or fallow, (5) piebald, (6) inferior qualities of all the foregoing. *Note:* A perfect piebald is preferable to a muddy brindle or defective solid color. Solid black is very undesirable, but not so objectionable if occurring to a moderate degree in piebald patches. The brindles to be perfect should have a fine, even and equal distribution of the composite colors. In brindles and solid colors a small white patch on the chest is not considered detrimental. In piebalds the color patches should be well defined, of pure color and symmetrically distributed.

Gait—The style and carriage are peculiar, his gait being a loose-jointed, shuffling, sidewise motion, giving the characteristic "roll." The action must, however, be unrestrained, free and vigorous.

Temperament—The disposition should be equable and kind, resolute and courageous (not vicious or aggressive), and demeanor should be pacific and dignified. These attributes should be countenanced by the expression and behavior.

Scale of Points

GENERAL PROPERTIES				
Proportion and symmetry	5		Jaws	5
Attitude	3		Teeth	2	39
Expression	2		BODY, LEGS, ETC.		
Gait	3		Neck	3
Size	3		Dewlap	2
Coat	2		Shoulders	5
Color of coat	4	22	Chest	3
HEAD			Ribs	3
Skull	5		Brisket	2
Cheeks	2		Belly	2
Stop	4		Back	5
Eyes and eyelids	3		Forelegs and elbows	4
Ears	5		Hind legs	3
Wrinkle	5		Feet	3
Nose	6		Tail	4	39
Chops	2		Total	100

Disqualification

Brown or liver-colored nose.

Approved July 20, 1976
Reformatted November 28, 1990

OFFICIAL STANDARD FOR THE CHINESE SHAR-PEI

General Appearance—An alert, dignified, active, compact dog of medium size and substance, square in profile, close-coupled, the well-proportioned head slightly but not overly large for the body. The short, harsh coat, the loose skin covering the head and body, the small ears, the "hippopotamus" muzzle shape and the high-set tail impart to the Shar-Pei a unique look peculiar to him alone. The loose skin and wrinkles covering the head, neck and body are superabundant in puppies but these features may be limited to the head, neck and withers in the adult.

Size, Proportion, Substance—The preferred *height* is 18 to 20 inches at the withers. The preferred *weight* is 40 to 55 pounds. The dog is usually larger and more square-bodied than the bitch but both appear well proportioned. *Proportion*—The height of the Shar-Pei from the ground to the withers is approximately equal to the length from the point of breastbone to the point of rump.

Head—Large, slightly but not overly proudly carried and covered with profuse wrinkles on the forehead continuing into side wrinkles framing the face. *Eyes*—Dark, small, almond-shaped and sunken, displaying a scowling expression. In the dilute-colored dogs the eye color may be lighter. *Ears*—Extremely small, rather thick, equilateral triangles in shape, slightly rounded at the tips, edges of the ear may curl. Ears lie flat against the head, are set wide apart and forward on the skull, pointing toward the eyes. The ears have the ability to move. Pricked ears are a disqualification. *Skull*—Flat and broad, the stop moderately defined. *Muzzle*—One of the distinctive features of the breed. It is broad and full with no suggestion of snipiness. (The length from nose to stop is approximately the same as from stop to occiput.) *Nose*—Large and wide and darkly pigmented, preferably black but any color nose conforming to the general coat color of the dog is acceptable. In dilute colors, the preferred nose is self-colored. Darkly pigmented cream Shar-Pei may have some light pigment either in the center of the nose or on the entire nose. The lips and top of muzzle are well padded and may cause a slight bulge at the base of the nose.

Tongue, Roof of Mouth, Gums and Flews—Solid bluish black is preferred in all coat colors except in dilute colors, which have a solid-lavender pigmentation. A spotted tongue is a major fault. A solid-pink tongue is a disqualification. (Tongue colors may lighten due to heat stress; care must be taken not to confuse dilute pigmentation with a pink tongue.) *Teeth*— Strong, meeting in a scissors bite. Deviation from a scissors bite is a major fault.

Neck, Topline, Body—*Neck*—Medium length, full and set well into the shoulders. There are moderate to heavy folds of loose skin and abundant dewlap about the neck and throat. *Topline*—The topline dips slightly behind the withers, slightly rising over the short, broad loin. *Chest*—Broad and deep with the brisket extending to the elbow and rising slightly under the loin. *Back*—Short and close-coupled. *Croup*—Flat, with the base of the tail set extremely high, clearly exposing an uptilted anus. *Tail*—The high-set tail is a characteristic feature of the Shar-Pei. The tail is thick and round at the base, tapering to a fine point and curling over or to either side of the back. The absence of a complete tail is a disqualification.

Forequarters—*Shoulders*—Muscular, well laid back and sloping. *Forelegs*—When viewed from the front, straight, moderately spaced, with elbows close to the body. When viewed from the side, the forelegs are straight, the pasterns are strong and flexible. The bone is substantial but never heavy and is of moderate length. Removal of front dewclaws is optional. *Feet*—Moderate in size, compact and firmly set, not splayed.

Hindquarters—Muscular, strong and moderately angulated. The metatarsi (hocks) are short, perpendicular to the ground and parallel to each other when viewed from the rear. Hind dewclaws must be removed. Feet as in front.

Coat—The extremely harsh coat is one of the distinguishing features of the breed. The coat is absolutely straight and offstanding on the main trunk of the body but generally lies somewhat flatter on the limbs. The coat appears healthy without being shiny or lustrous. Acceptable coat lengths may range from extremely short "horse coat" up to the "brush coat," not to exceed one inch in length at the withers. A soft coat, a wavy coat, a coat in excess of 1 inch in length at the withers or a coat that has been trimmed is a major fault. The Shar-Pei is shown in its natural state.

Color—Only solid colors are acceptable. A solid-colored dog may have shading, primarily darker down the back and on the ears. The shading must be variations of the same body color (except in sables) and may include darker hairs throughout the coat. The following colors are a disqualifying fault:

Not a solid color, i.e.: Albino; Brindle; Parti-colored (patches); Spotted (including spots, ticked or roaning); Tan-Pointed Pattern (including typical black and tan or saddled patterns).

Gait—The movement of the Shar-Pei is to be judged at a trot. The gait is free and balanced with the feet tending to converge on a center line of gravity when the dog moves at a vigorous trot. The gait combines good forward reach and a strong drive in the hindquarters. Proper movement is essential.

Temperament—Regal, alert, intelligent, dignified, lordly, scowling, sober and snobbish, essentially independent and somewhat standoffish with strangers, but extreme in his devotion to his family. The Shar-Pei stands firmly on the ground with a calm, confident stature.

Major Faults

Deviation from a scissors bite.
Spotted tongue.
A soft coat, a wavy coat, a coat in excess of 1 inch in length at the withers or a coat that has been trimmed.

Disqualifications

Pricked ears.
Solid-pink tongue.

Absence of a complete tail.

Not a solid color, i.e.: albino; brindle, parti-colored (patches); spotted (including spots, ticked or roaning); tan-pointed pattern (including typical black and tan or saddled patterns).

Approved October 8, 1991

Lemon Laws

Lemon laws are consumer protection legislation, most often on the local level when it comes to dogs. Though there was an attempt in 1992 to pass federal legislation of this nature under the misnamed "Puppy Protection Act." Thanks to the concerted efforts of the fancy, it was soundly defeated.

The underlying intent of this type of legislation is to protect the public from the big, bad breeder. Note that they do not say the irresponsible breeder or back-yard breeder. While they were originally aimed at pet store and other commercial operations, these lemon laws are starting to have an impact on the small hobby breeder.

These laws are well-kept secrets that only appear when a complaint has been filed with the local consumer affairs office. Then they rear their ugly heads and few people challenge their application.

For example, the New Jersey Consumer Protection Act contains a Sale of Animals section. When this was enacted in the 1970s there was discussion at several local club meetings concerning its requirements, implications and potential impact on the small breeder. A number of the more active breeders had signs made, information printed, contracts revised, etc. A number of breeders were fined under the act and no one challenged it. Of course, no one had a copy of the whole act nor was much research devoted to the matter. Many years later, several of my clients were faced with this lemon law as well as a proposed task force to spot-check and monitor breeder compliance with its provisions. Finally, I read the entire text and, lo and behold, it does not apply to private breeders, a fact that was further substantiated by case law.

Does this mean that New Jersey breeders were stupid in the 1970s? No, not necessarily. We were, like other fanciers and breeders throughout the United States, feeling safe in our own little world and taking care of the priorities as we saw them at that time. This was not a particularly threatening piece of legislation. Also, the fact that it was already in place by the time we learned of its existence led us to believe that there was little, if anything, we could do except conform to the situation.

Even today, dog people have a tendency to conform to outside influences. For example, a local municipality recently proposed an ordinance under which owners would be limited to four dogs per residence, puppies would have to be gone from the property no later than eight weeks of age and any frequent or continuous barking heard across a property line would be prohibited. Fines were hefty (up to $1,000) and imprisonment for not more than six months could be imposed. In addition, each day a violation of the ordinance occurred was considered a separate offense. Due to the large turnout of people opposed to this ordinance at the public meeting, a committee was formed to review the ordinance and make recommendations. Only one person on the committee raised the issue of trying to have the whole ordinance tabled. The dog people were more concerned about the enforcement of the ordinance and allowed it to pass in an amended form.

Let us consider the pertinent sections of the New Jersey lemon law on dogs.

13:45A-12.1   Definitions

The following words and terms, when used in this subchapter, shall have the following meanings, unless the context clearly indicates otherwise:

"Animal" means a dog or cat.

"Consumer" means any natural person purchasing a dog or cat from a pet dealer.

"Division" means the Division of Consumer Affairs, Department of Law and Public Safety.

"Kennel" means the business of boarding dogs or cats or breeding dogs or cats for sale.

"Person" means any person as defined by N.J.S.A. 56:8-1(d).

"Pet dealer" means any person engaged in the ordinary course of business in the sale of animals for profit to the public.

"Pet shop" means the business of selling, offering for sale or exposing for sale dogs or cats.

"Quarantine" means to hold in segregation from the general animal population any dog or cat because of the presence or suspected presence of a contagious or infectious disease.

"Unfit for purchase" means any disease, deformity, injury, physical condition, illness or defect which is congenital or hereditary and severely affects the health of the animal, or which was manifest, capable of diagnosis or likely to have been contracted on or before the sale and delivery of the animal to the consumer. The death of an animal within 14 days of its delivery to the consumer, except death by accident or as a result of injuries sustained during that period shall mean such animal was unfit for purchase.

13:45A-12.2   General provisions

(a) Without limiting the prosecution of any other practices which may be unlawful under N.J.S.A. 56:8-1 et seq., the following acts, practices or omissions shall be deceptive practices in the conduct of the business of a pet dealer:

1. To sell an animal within the State of New Jersey without an animal history and health certificate and without providing the consumer with a completed animal history and health certificate. The animal history and health certificate shall be signed by the pet dealer, his agent or employee, and shall contain the following information:

i. The animal's breed, sex, age, color, and birth date;

ii. The name and address of the person from whom the pet dealer purchased the animal;

iii. The breeder's name and address, and the litter number of the animal;

iv. The name and registration number of the animal's sire and dam;

v. The date the pet dealer took possession of the animal;

vi. The date the animal was shipped to the pet dealer, where such date is known by the dealer;

vii. The date or dates on which the animal was examined by a veterinarian licensed to practice in the State of New Jersey, the name and address of such veterinarian, the findings made and the treatment, if any, taken or given to the animal;

  viii. A statement of all vaccinations and inoculations administered to the animal, including the identity and quantity of the vaccine or inoculum administered, the name and address of the person or licensed veterinarian administering the same, and the date of administering the vaccinations and inoculations; and

    ix. A 10-point bold-face type warning in the following form:

WARNING

The animal which you have purchased (check one) ☐ has ☐ has not been previously vaccinated or inoculated. Vaccination or inoculation neither guarantees good health nor assures absolute immunity against disease. Examination by a veterinarian is essential at the earliest possible date to enable your veterinarian to insure the good health of your pet.

  2. To fail to maintain a copy of the animal history and health certificate signed by the consumer for a period of one year following the date of sale and/or to fail to permit inspection thereof by an authorized representative of the Division upon two days' notice (exclusive of Saturday and Sunday).

  3. To include in the animal history and health certificate any false or misleading statement.

  4. To directly or indirectly refer, promote, suggest, recommend or advise that a consumer consult with, use, seek or obtain the services of a licensed veterinarian unless the consumer is provided with the names of not less than three licensed veterinarians of whom only one may be the veterinarian retained by the pet dealer for its purposes.

  5. To describe or promote the operation of the business as a "kennel" unless the business operation falls within the definition contained in N.J.A.C. 13:45A-12.1 or the operation of the business as a "kennel" has been authorized by the issuance of a license pursuant to N.J.S.A. 4:19-15.8. In the absence of meeting such criteria, a pet dealer shall be considered to be engaged in the operation of a "pet shop" and shall, where the name for the business operation includes the word "kennel," indicate the following disclaimer in proximate location to the name for the business operation in all promotional or advertising activities:

  "This business only engages in the operation of a pet shop."

  6. To use or employ a name for the business operation which suggests or implies that such business operation is engaged in or is associated with any organization which registers or certifies the pedigree or lineage of animals and/or to represent, expressly or by implication, approval by or affiliation with such organization, unless the following disclaimer, as

appropriate, appears in proximate location to the name for the business operation:

"This business only engages in the operation of a pet shop."

"This business only engages in the operation of a kennel."

7. To state, promise or represent, directly or indirectly, that an animal is registered or capable of being registered with an animal pedigree registry organization, followed by a failure either to effect such registration or provide the consumer with the documents necessary therefor 120 days following the date of sale of such animal. In the event that a pet dealer fails to effect registration or to provide the necessary documents within 120 days following the date of sale, the consumer shall, upon written notice to the pet dealer, be entitled to choose one of the following options:

i. To return the animal and to receive a refund of the purchase price plus sales tax; or

ii. To retain the animal and to receive a partial refund of 75 percent of the purchase price plus sales tax.

8. A pet dealer's failure to comply with the consumer's election pursuant to (a)7 above within 10 days of written notice thereof shall be deemed a separate deceptive practice for purposes of this section.

9. To fail to display conspicuously on the business premises a sign not smaller than 22 inches by 18 inches which clearly states to the public in letters no less than one inch high the following:

KNOW YOUR RIGHTS

The sale of dogs and cats is subject to a regulation of the New Jersey Division of Consumer Affairs. Read your animal history and health certificate, the Statement of New Jersey Law Governing the Sale of Dogs and Cats and your Contract. In the event of a complaint you may contact: Division of Consumer Affairs, 1100 Raymond Boulevard, Newark, New Jersey 07102. (201) 648-3622.

(b) It shall be a deceptive practice within the meaning of this section for a pet dealer to secure or attempt to secure a waiver of any of the provisions contained in (a) above.

13:45A-12.3 Required practices related to the health of animals and fitness for sale and purchase

(a) Without limiting the prosecution of any other practices which may be unlawful under N.J.S.A. 56:8-1 et seq., it shall be a deceptive practice for a pet dealer to sell animals within the State of New Jersey without complying with the following minimum standards relating to the health of animals and fitness for sale and purchase:

1. A pet dealer shall have each animal examined by a veterinarian licensed to practice in the State of New Jersey prior to the sale of the animal. The name and address of the examining veterinarian, together with the findings made and treatment (if any) ordered as a result of the examination, shall be noted on each animal's history and health certificate as required by N.J.A.C. 13:45A-12.2(a)1vii.
2. A pet dealer shall label and identify each cage as to the:
  i. Sex and breed of animal;
  ii. Date and place of birth of each animal; and
  iii. Name and address of the attending licensed New Jersey veterinarian and the date of initial examination.
3. A pet dealer shall be required to quarantine any animal diagnosed as suffering from a contagious or infectious disease, illness or condition until such time as a licensed New Jersey veterinarian determines that such animal is free from contagion or infection. All animals requiring quarantining shall be placed in a quarantine area separated from the general animal population.
4. A pet dealer shall be permitted to inoculate and vaccinate animals prior to purchase only on the order of a veterinarian licensed to practice in the State of New Jersey. A pet dealer, however, shall be prohibited from representing, directly or indirectly, that he is qualified to engage in or is engaging in, directly or indirectly, the following activities: diagnosing, prognosing, treating, administering, prescribing, operating on, manipulating or applying any apparatus or appliance for disease, pain, deformity, defect, injury, wound or physical condition of animals after purchase for the prevention of, or to test for, the presence of any disease in such animals. These prohibitions include but are not limited to the giving of inoculations or vaccinations after purchase, the diagnosing, prescribing and dispersing of medication to animals and the prescribing of any diet or dietary supplement as treatment for any disease, pain, deformity, defect, injury, wound or physical condition.
5. A pet dealer shall have any animal which has been examined more than 14 days prior to purchase reexamined by a licensed New Jersey veterinarian for the purpose of disclosing its condition at the time of purchase. Such examination shall take place within 72 hours of delivery of the animal to the consumer unless the consumer waives this right to reexamination in writing. The written waiver shall be in the following form and a copy shall be given to the consumer prior to the signing of any contract or agreement to purchase the animal:

KNOW YOUR RIGHTS

To ensure that healthy animals are sold in this State, New Jersey law requires that a dog or cat be examined by a licensed New Jersey veterinarian prior to its sale by a pet dealer and within 72 hours of the delivery of the dog or cat to a consumer who has purchased the animal where the initial examination took place more than 14 days prior to the date of purchase. A pet dealer need not have the animal reexamined if you, the consumer, decide that you do not want such a reexamination performed.

If you do not want a reexamination performed, please indicate your decision below.

WAIVER OF REEXAMINATION RIGHT

I understand that I have the right to have my animal reexamined within 72 hours of its delivery to me. I do not want to have such a reexamination performed.

Consumer's Name
(Print)

Consumer's Signature

Date

Pet Dealer's or Agent's
Name (Indicate Title or
Position)
(Print)

Pet Dealer's or Agent's
Signature

Date

6. If at any time within 14 days following the sale and delivery of an animal to a consumer, a licensed veterinarian certifies such animal to be unfit for purchase due to a non-congenital cause or condition or within six months certifies an animal to be unfit for purchase due to a congenital or hereditary cause or condition, a consumer shall have the right to elect one of the following options:

i. The right to return the animal and receive a refund of the purchase price, including sales tax, plus reimbursement of the veterinary fees incurred prior to the consumer's receipt of the veterinary certification. The pet dealer's liability for veterinary fees under this option shall not exceed a dollar amount equal to the purchase price, including sales tax, of the animal;

ii. The right to retain the animal and to receive reimbursement for veterinary fees incurred prior to the consumer's receipt of the veterinary certification, plus the future cost of veterinary fees to be incurred in curing or attempting to cure the animal. The pet dealer's liability under this option shall not exceed a dollar amount equal to the purchase price, including sales tax, of the animal;

iii. The right to return the animal and to receive in exchange an animal of the consumer's choice, of equivalent value, plus reimbursement of veterinary fees incurred prior to the consumer's receipt of the veterinary certification. The pet dealer's liability for veterinary fees under this option shall not exceed a dollar amount equal to the purchase price, including sales tax, of the animal;

iv. In the event of the animal's death within 14 days of its delivery to the consumer, except where death occurs by accident or injury sustained during that period, the right to receive a full refund of the purchase price plus sales tax for the animal, or in exchange an animal of the consumer's choice of equivalent value, plus reimbursement of veterinary fees incurred prior to the death of the animal. The pet dealer's liability for veterinary fees under this option shall not exceed a dollar amount equal to the purchase price, including sales tax, of the animal.

7. The pet dealer shall accept receipt of a veterinary certification of unfitness which has been delivered by the consumer within five days following the consumer's receipt thereof, such certification to contain the following information:

i. The name of the owner;

ii. The date or dates of examination;

iii. The breed, color, sex and age of the animal;

iv. A statement of the veterinarian's findings;

v. A statement that the veterinarian certifies the animal to be "unfit for purchase";

vi. An itemized statement of veterinary fees incurred as of the date of the certification;

vii. Where the animal is curable, the estimated fee to cure the animal;

viii. Where the animal has died, a statement setting forth the probable cause of death; and

ix. The name and address of the certifying veterinarian and the date of the certification.

8. When a consumer presents a veterinary certification of unfitness to the pet dealer, the pet dealer shall confirm the consumer's election in writing. The election shall be in the following form and a copy shall be given to the consumer upon signing:

UNFITNESS OF ANIMAL—ELECTION OF OPTION

I understand that, upon delivery of my veterinarian's certification of unfitness, I have the right to elect one of the following options. I am aware of those options and I understand each of them. I have chosen the following option:

☐ 1. Return of my animal and receipt of a refund of the purchase price, including sales tax for the animal, plus reimbursement of the veterinary fees incurred prior to the date I received my veterinarian's certification of unfitness. The reimbursement for veterinarian's fees shall not exceed a dollar amount equal to the purchase price including sales tax of my animal.

☐ 2. Retention of my animal and reimbursement for the veterinary fees incurred prior to the date I received my veterinarian's certification of unfitness, plus the future cost to be incurred in curing or attempting to cure my animal. The total reimbursement for veterinarian's fees shall not exceed a dollar amount equal to the purchase price including sales tax for my animal.

☐ 3. Return of my animal and receipt of an animal of my choice of equivalent value in exchange plus reimbursement of veterinary fees incurred prior to the date I received my veterinarian's certification of unfitness. The reimbursement for veterinarian's fees shall not exceed a dollar amount equal to the purchase price including sales tax of my animal.

☐ 4. DEATH OF ANIMAL ONLY. (check one) ☐ Receipt of a full refund of the purchase price, including sales tax for the animal, or in exchange an animal of my choice of equivalent value plus reimbursement of the veterinary fees incurred prior to the death of the animal. The reimbursement for veterinarian's fees shall not exceed a dollar amount equal to the purchase price including sales tax of my animal.

_____   _____
Consumer's Name   Consumer's Signature
(Print)

                                     _____
                                     Date

_____   _____
Pet Dealer's or Agent's   Pet Dealer's or Agent's
Name (Indicate Title or   Signature
Position)
(Print)
                                     _____
                                     Date

9. A pet dealer shall comply with the consumer's election as required by (a)7i through iv above not later than 10 days following receipt of a

133

veterinary certification. In the event that a pet dealer wishes to contest a consumer's election, he shall notify the consumer and the Director of the Division of Consumer Affairs in writing within five days following the receipt of the veterinarian's certification, and he may require the consumer to produce the animal for examination by a veterinarian of the dealer's choice at a mutually convenient time and place. The Director shall, upon receipt of such notice, provide a hearing pursuant to the Administrative Procedure Act, N.J.S.A. 52:14B-1 et seq., and the Uniform Administrative Procedure Rules, N.J.A.C. 1:1, to determine why the option elected by the consumer should not be allowed.

10. A pet dealer shall give the following written notice to a consumer prior to the delivery of the animal. Such notice, signed by both the pet dealer and the consumer, shall be embodied in a separate document and shall state the following in 10 point boldface type:

KNOW YOUR RIGHTS—A STATEMENT OF NEW JERSEY LAW GOVERNING THE SALE OF DOGS AND CATS

The sale of dogs and cats is subject to a regulation of the New Jersey Division of Consumer Affairs. In the event that a licensed veterinarian certifies your animal to be unfit for purchase within 14 days following receipt of your animal or within six months in the case of a congenital or hereditary cause or condition, you may:

i. Return your animal and receive a refund of the purchase price including sales tax; or

ii. Keep your animal and attempt to cure it; or

iii. Return your animal and receive an animal of your choice of equivalent value.

Further, in the event of your animal's death within this 14-day period, except where death occurs by accident or as a result of injuries sustained after delivery, you may choose to receive either a full refund of the purchase price plus sales tax or an animal of your choice of equivalent value. In addition, veterinary fees limited to the purchase price, including sales tax, of the animal must be paid by the pet dealer.

In order to exercise these rights, you must present to the pet dealer a written veterinary certification that the animal is unfit for purchase and an itemized bill of all veterinary fees incurred prior to your receipt of the certification. Both of these items must be presented no later than five days after you have received the certification of unfitness. In the event that the pet dealer wishes to contest the certification or the bill, he may request a hearing at the Division of Consumer Affairs. If the pet dealer does not contest the matter, he must make the refund or reimbursement not later than ten days after receiving the veterinary certification.

Although your dog or cat is required to be examined by a licensed New Jersey veterinarian prior to sale, symptoms of certain conditions may not appear until after sale. If your dog or cat appears ill, you should have it examined by a licensed veterinarian of your choice at the earliest possible time.

If the pet dealer has promised to register your animal or to provide the necessary papers and fails to do so within 120 days following the date of sale, you are entitled to return the animal and receive a full refund of the purchase price plus sales tax or to keep the animal and receive a refund of 75 percent of the purchase price plus sales tax.

11. It shall be a deceptive practice within the meaning of this section for a pet dealer to secure or attempt to secure a waiver of any of the provisions of this section except as specifically authorized under (a)6 above.

The first step in analyzing this or any other statute or ordinance is to read the Definitions section to see who exactly it applies to before jumping to conclusions based upon the words "dog," "animals," "pets," etc. Here the application is to dogs and cats. While "person" is defined under another statute, which you can look up later, there are separate definitions for "kennel," "pet dealer" and "pet shop." In addition, the drafters obviously felt that the terms "quarantine" and "unfit for purchase" were important enough or were used often enough to be defined in the first section.

Note that both "kennel" and "pet shop" use the term "means the business of," while "pet dealer" uses the phrase "in the ordinary course of business." Note also the broad definition of "unfit for purchase."

Now look at the first paragraph of the General Provisions section. This states that "the following acts, practices, or omissions shall be deceptive practices in the conduct of the business of a pet dealer." The operative words here are "pet dealer." Look again at the definition of a pet dealer and note again the reference to the ordinary course of business.

By definition, the ordinary course of business refers to an activity that is normal and incidental to the business. Occasional isolated or casual transactions are not frequent or continuous enough to constitute the ordinary course of business. In sales, the ordinary course of business refers to property usually for sale to customers of the trade.

Further support for this is found in case law, where the courts have refused to apply this act to any private operation, including that of a private utility. Thus, in view of the use of the phrase "ordinary course of business" and the courts' policy of restricting the act's application only to commercial enterprises, the private breeder should not fall within its operation.

Further into this provision are four remedies that the consumer may elect. They could be devastating to a small hobby breeder. Regrettably, a number of veterinarians have taken it upon themselves to suggest, in their letters stating the results of hip X-rays, that the owner should contact the Division of Consumer Affairs.

Although they act slowly, if you are contacted by a consumer affairs investigator or director, see an attorney immediately. Some of the people in these positions are quite militant and will not listen to reason. They also have no conception of the specialization of modern veterinary medicine. Never doubt that, whether right or wrong, informed or misinformed, a consumers affairs office will proceed to right whatever perceived wrong has been done to a consumer who files a complaint with them.

Finally, check to see if your area has a lemon law that is applicable to dogs or has been applied in the past. If you don't have one, be aware that it may appear in the near future. After breed-specific legislation, the lemon law as we have it today is probably the worst piece of legislation on the books if it affects, has the potential to affect or is aimed at the private hobby breeder. Remember that while they may be appropriately aimed at the real problems in dogdom, there may still be potential problems in their application.

Breeding Bans

The latest in proposed legislation directed at dogs and dog people is the total breeding ban within a geographical area, the suggested moratorium for a specific period of time or the requirement of high licensing fees for breeders and/or litter fees of more than $100 each.

The perceived problem being targeted is pet overpopulation. Regardless of the statistical fact that the purebred population in shelters has declined, that more and more dogs are being placed rather than destroyed, the advocates of these banning/restricting scenarios are adamant that we, the purebred fancier and breeder, are the problem to be solved.

San Mateo, California, actually passed a breeding ban within its city limits. While that has since been modified, a number of other communities are considering, or have already considered, the same thing. However, this time we were a little better prepared and met the attack head-on.

There was a concerted effort in New Jersey, on a statewide basis, by People for the Ethical Treatment of Animals (PETA) to enact such legislation. To date, nothing of that nature has occurred. So when that did not work in the various states, the next step was to have the Humane Society of the United States call for a voluntary breeding moratorium for a one- to two-year period. These people are not stupid and this sounds like a workable solution. What is not taken into account is the potential impact on the individual, the pet industry and many other concerned entities over the long term. Now they are trying to have a mandatory breeding moratorium put into effect.

The outcome and ultimate impact of this is yet to be seen. However, we all need to be aware that this is the next in a series of attempts to restrict dogs and dog owners, and we should be prepared to fight the passage of local, state and federal legislation.

I have not discussed the particulars on how to introduce, defeat or enact legislation, as this has already been handled in a booklet entitled *The Legislative Action Manual* by Janice Mullen-Stewart, which is available from the American Kennel Club.

Senate Bill 1158

66th Oregon Legislative Assembly -- 1991 Regular Session

A BILL FOR AN ACT

Relating to animal control.

Be It Enacted by the People of the State of Oregon:

SECTION 1. (1) Any person who keeps companion animals and sells or offers to sell more than one litter of puppies or other companion animals in any one calendar year, or who keeps such animals for breeding, must obtain a license annually from the State Department of Agriculture pursuant to the following:

(a) The annual licensing fee shall be $150.

(b) A fee of $200 per litter shall be required for the sale of each complete litter.

(c) A license application fee of $150 shall be paid for each companion animal six months old or older owned by the applicant.

(2) Any person who acts or attempts to act as a companion animal broker must obtain an annual license from the State Department of Agriculture and shall pay an annual licensing fee therefor of $1,500.

SECTION 2. (1) Any person who houses companion animals for the purpose of selling or breeding such animals and who is licensed as prescribed in section 1 of this Act shall:

(a) Provide at least one staff person for every five adult animals;

(b) Insure that there is a minimum of 3,000 square feet of ground area for every 10 adult animals, with no more than 10 adult animals occupying such area at any one time;

(c) Insure that all animals are provided adequate food and water in containers that are cleaned and disinfected daily. Water shall be provided at least every 12 hours;

(d) Insure that no more than three separate breeds of dogs are kept simultaneously;

(e) Insure that no bitch has more than one litter every other year and that no puppy under 12 weeks old is sold;

(f) Insure that each animal is examined by a licensed veterinarian at least every six months, with verification to be filed with the State Department of Agriculture; and

(g) Insure that each animal has adequate housing, including but not limited to:

(A) Elevation of the structure above the ground sufficient to prevent dampness;

(B) Waterproofing and insulation of each structure;

(C) Sheltered entrances on all structures;

(D) Interior space in each structure that allows the animal freedom of movement while being small enough to retain natural body heat;

(E) Straw, hay or other acceptable bedding to be changed daily; and

(F) Solid floors not slatted or made of wire in all structures.

(2) The State Department of Agriculture or its designee shall inspect the housing arrangements of all animals kept by persons licensed under this Act for compliance with the provisions of this section.

SECTION 3. (1) Failure to obtain the necessary license required by this Act before engaging in keeping, breeding, selling or brokering companion animals is a Class C felony.

(2) Buying or selling or offering for sale puppies by the litter lot is a Class C felony.

(3) Debarking or causing the debarking of a dog is a Class C felony.

(4) Failure to comply with any of the provisions of this Act by an applicant for a license is cause to deny a license application.

(5) Failure to comply with any of the provisions of this Act by a licensed person is cause to permanently revoke that person's license and confiscate all companion animals being kept by that person. Such licensed person in violation shall pay a fine of $10 per day per confiscated animal until such confiscated animals are placed or otherwise disposed of.

SECTION 4. For the purposes of this Act, "companion animal" or "animal" means any animal kept by a person, business or other entity for companionship, security, hunting, herding or providing assistance in relation to a physical disability.

It would be a simple matter for certain kinds of competitions or demonstrations, such as weight-pulling, to be considered instances of cruelty even if they are not. Recent legislation, however, have been put in place that protect the dogs participating, their owners, spectators and those in charge of organizing these events.

13

Cruelty Legislation and Agencies

CRUELTY to animals is against the law. However, what constitutes cruelty and how it is handled varies from one area to another. Most cases of cruelty are treated as misdemeanors or disorder-person offenses. The exception is dog fighting, which may be indictable.

One good effect that has come from the increased scrutiny and legislation with respect to dogs and dog owners is the strengthening of the anti-cruelty statutes. Below is a recent ammendment to the New Jersey statute. Note the underlined sections which have been added or changed. Many of these changes have been hailed by the dog world, including the recognition of organized activities that once were probably considered cruelty under vague definitions contained in the statute (e.g., Weight Pulling demonstrations/competitions). They have also recognized the training of service dogs. The methods by which dogs may be euthanized have also been addressed, and the penalties for abandoning an animal to die in a public place have been increased. The definition of people who may be charged under the dog fighting section has been expanded.

However, it is still up to the Society for the Prevention of

141

Cruelty to Animals to enforce these laws. The Society consists of state and local organizations. Some are better than others. The enabling statutes are rather broad and allow the organizations to enact their own rules and regulations. A proposed improvement to enable the certified Animal Control Officers, after additional training, to enforce the cruelty laws would be a big improvement.

The main problem, here and in other areas, is the lack of a set procedure, consistency within each organization and public awareness of how to proceed when a potential violation is observed. In addition, many groups (e.g., PETA) have their own agenda, which has little, if anything, to do with cruelty problems.

Shelters are in the same situation. Some are good and some are bad. Just because a shelter calls itself a humane society shelter does not mean it is affiliated with or governed by the Humane Society of the United States. Unless shelters are regulated locally, anyone can set one up.

For more information about the direction of the humane movement in the United States, read *The Hijacking of the Humane Movement* by Rod and Patti Strand. There is more going on in these organizations than meets the eye, and dog owners keep sending their money into a variety of groups, some of which we would not support if we only knew their real agenda.

There is a considerable and critical difference between animal rights and animal welfare.

PREVENTION OF CRUELTY TO ANIMALS

ARTICLE 2. PREVENTION OF CRUELTY

B. MISDEMEANOR AND FINES

D. ARRESTS, SEARCHES, SEIZURES, ETC.

ARTICLE 2. PREVENTION OF CRUELTY

A. DEFINITIONS; CONSTRUCTION

4:22–16. Construction of article

Nothing contained in this article shall be construed to prohibit or interfere with:

a. Properly conducted scientific experiments performed under the authority of the State Department of Health. That department may authorize the conduct of such experiments or investigations by agricultural stations and schools maintained by the State or federal government, or by medical societies, universities, colleges and philanthropic institutions incorporated or authorized to do business in this State and having among their corporate purposes investigation into the causes, nature, prevention and cure of diseases in men and animals; and may for cause revoke such authority;

b. The killing or disposing of an animal or creature by virtue of the order of a constituted authority of the State;

c. The shooting or taking of game or game fish in such manner and at such times as is allowed or provided by the laws of this State;

d. The training or engaging of a dog to accomplish a task or participate in an activity or exhibition designed to develop the physical or mental characteristics of that dog. These activities shall be carried out in accordance with the practices, guidelines or rules established by an organization founded for the purpose of promoting and enhancing working dog activities or exhibitions; in a manner which does not adversely affect the health or safety of the dog; and may include avalanche warning, guide work, obedience work, carting, dispatching, freight racing, packing, sled dog racing, sledding, tracking, and weight pull demonstrations.

Amended by L.1985, c. 433, § 1, eff. Jan. 13, 1986.

As amended by the Assembly Agriculture and Environment Committee, Assembly Bill No. 1509 would stipulate the criteria under which certain dog races or exhibitions may take place: to wit, by the International Sled Dog Racing Association, its affiliates or other similar organizations which are nonprofit and have been in existence for five years or more, with animals which have been trained for these purposes, and under conditions that are humane and not inconsistent with the laws against cruelty.

The committee amended the bill to amend R.S. 4:22–16, clarifying that the laws against cruelty to animals would not be construed to prohibit the training or engaging of dogs for these races or exhibitions as long as they were held under humane conditions.

The committee also amended the bill to repeal R.S. 4:22–25 which states, in essence, that using a dog to draw a vehicle for business or other purposes would subject the violator to a $1.00 fine for the first offense and to a $10.00 fine for each subsequent offense. R.S. 4:22–26 presently provides a $250.00 fine for the use of a dog in drawing a vehicle for business purposes and the amendment to 4:22–25 suggested in the bill would have established different penalties for identical violations.

B. MISDEMEANORS AND FINES

4:22–17. Cruelty in general; misdemeanor

4:22–18. Carrying animal in cruel manner; misdemeanor

4:22–19. Failure to care for or destruction of impounded animals; penalties; collection

A person who shall:

a. Impound or confine, or cause to be impounded or confined, in a pound or other place, a living animal or creature, and shall fail to supply it during such confinement with a sufficient quantity of good and wholesome food and water; or

b. Destroy or cause to be destroyed any such animal by hypoxia induced by decompression or in any other manner, by the administration of a lethal gas other than an inhalant anesthetic, or in any other manner except by a method of euthanasia generally accepted by the veterinary medical profession as being reliable, appropriate to the type of animal upon which it is to be employed, and capable of producing loss of consciousness and death as rapidly and painlessly as possible for such animal shall, in the case of a violation of paragraph subsection a., be guilty of a misdemeanor and punished as provided in section 4:22-17 of this Title disorderly persons offense; or, in the case of a violation of paragraph subsection b., be subject to a penalty of $25.00 for the first offense and $50.00 for each subsequent offense. Each animal destroyed in violation of paragraph subsection b. shall constitute a separate offense. The penalty shall be collected in accordance with "the penalty enforcement law" (N. J. S. 2A:58–1 et seq.) and all money collected shall be remitted to the State.

Paragraphs a. and b. of this This section shall apply to kennels, pet shops, shelters and pounds as defined and licensed pursuant to P.L.1941, c. 151 (C. 4:19–15.1 et seq.); to pounds and places of confinement owned and operated by municipalities, counties or regional governmental authorities; and to every contractual warden or impounding service, any provision to the contrary in this title notwithstanding.

Amended by L.1977, c. 231, § 1, eff. Sept. 20, 1977; L.1982, c. 76, § 1, eff. July 22, 1982; L.1982, c. 158, § 2, eff. Oct. 27, 1982.

4:22–19.1. Chamber or device to induce hypoxia; dismantlement and removal

Within 30 days of the effective date of this act, any chamber or device used to induce hypoxia through decompression or in any other manner shall be dismantled and removed from the premises. The owner of any premises on which the chamber or device remains 30 days subsequent to the effective date of this act shall be guilty of a disorderly persons offense.

L.1982, c. 76, § 3, eff. July 22, 1982.

For similar section added by L. 1982, c. 158, § 3, eff. Oct. 27, 1982, see § 4:22–19.2, post.

4:22–19.2. Dismantlement and removal of decompression chamber or device; offense

Within 30 days of the effective date of this act, any chamber or device used to induce hypoxia through decompression or in any other manner and any gas chamber or similar device, except one which is used for the administration of an inhalant anesthetic, shall be dismantled and removed from the premises. The owner of any premises on which the chamber or device remains 30 days subsequent to the effective date of this act shall be guilty of a disorderly persons offense.

L.1982, c. 158, § 3, eff. Oct. 27, 1982.

For similar section added by L. 1982, c. 76, § 3, eff. July 22, 1982, see § 4:22–19.1, ante.

4:22–19.3. Prohibition of use of neuromuscular blocking agent to destroy domestic animal

Whenever any dog, cat, or any other domestic animal is to be destroyed, the use of succinylcholine chloride, curare, curariform drugs, or any other substance which acts as a neuromuscular blocking agent is prohibited.

L.1988, c. 160, § 1, eff. Nov. 16, 1988.

Assembly Committee on Conservation, Natural Resources and Energy Statement

Assembly, No. 697—L.1988, c. 160

The Assembly Committee on Conservation, Natural Resources and Energy favorably reported Assembly Bill No. 697 with amendments.

As amended by the committee, the bill would ban the use of neuromuscular blocking agents for destroying animals. Violators would be subject to a penalty of $25 for the first offense and $50 for each subsequent offense. Each animal destroyed would constitute a separate offense.

This bill was pre-filed for introduction in the 1988 session pending technical review. As reported the bill includes the changes required by technical review, which has been performed.

4:22–19.4. Violations; penalty

A person who violates this act shall be subject to a penalty of $25.00 for the first offense and $50.00 for each subsequent offense, to be collected in a civil action by a summary proceeding under "the penalty enforcement law" (N.J.S. 2A:58–1 et seq.). Each animal destroyed in violation of this act shall constitute a separate offense. The Superior Court shall have jurisdiction to enforce "the penalty enforcement law."

L.1988, c. 160, § 2, eff. Nov. 16, 1988.

4:22–20. Abandoning disabled animal to die in public place; abandoning domesticated animal; disorderly persons offense

a. A person who shall abandon a maimed, sick, infirm or disabled animal or creature to die in a public place, shall be guilty of a disorderly persons offense.

b. A person who shall abandon a domesticated animal shall be guilty of a disorderly persons offense. The violator shall be subject to the maximum $1,000 penalty.

Amended by L.1977, c. 229, § 1, eff. Sept. 20, 1977; L.1986, c. 176, § 1, eff. Dec. 8, 1986; L.1991, c. 108, § 1, eff. April 19, 1991.

Assembly Energy and Natural Resources Committee Statement

Assembly, No. 635—L.1986, c. 176

The Committee favorably reported Assembly Bill No. 635. This bill increases the fine for abandoning maimed, sick, infirm or disabled animals or creatures in a public place, or cats or dogs. A person violating this statute is subject to a fine of not more than $250.00 or imprisonment for a term not to exceed six months, or both. This bill would increase the fine to not more than $1,000.00 and expand the scope of the prohibition to include domesticated animals.

4:22–21. Sale of horses unfit for work; misdemeanor

4:22–22. Use or disposal of animals having transmissible diseases; misdemeanor

4:22–23. Use of live birds as targets; misdemeanor

4:22–24. Fighting or baiting animals or creatures and related offenses

A person who shall:

a. Keep, use, be connected with or interested in the management of, or receive money for the admission of a person to, a place kept or used for the purpose of fighting or baiting a living animal or creature;

b. Be present and witness, pay admission to, encourage or assist therein; or

c. Permit or suffer a place owned or controlled by him to be so used;

d. For amusement or gain, cause, allow, or permit the fighting or baiting of a living animal or creature;

e. Own, possess, keep, train, promote, purchase, or knowingly sell a living animal or creature for the purpose of fighting or baiting that animal or creature; or

f. Gamble on the outcome of a fight involving a living animal or creature—

Shall be guilty of a crime of the third degree.

Amended by L.1989, c. 35, § 1, eff. March 7, 1989.

Assembly Conservation, Natural Resources and Energy Committee Statement

Assembly, No. 1416—L. 1989, c. 35

A–1416 is reported favorably by the committee.

This bill would upgrade the offense of keeping a place for, witnessing, or encouraging the fighting or baiting of living animals or creatures from a crime of the fourth degree to a crime of the third degree. The jail term for a conviction therefor would thus increase from the present maximum of 18 months to between three and five years. The fine would continue to be a maximum of $7,500. The bill would also expand criminal liability under the animal fighting act to encompass those who cause, allow, or permit the fighting or baiting of a living animal or creature, who keep, train, promote, purchase, or knowingly sell animals for the purpose of fighting or baiting them, or who gamble on the outcome of these fights. The bill would permit the New Jersey Society for the Prevention of Cruelty of Animals to bring a civil action against any person engaging in these activities. Finally, the bill provides that the costs of sheltering, caring for, treating, and, if necessary, destroying a seized animal or creature be borne by the owner thereof.

This bill was pre-filed for introduction in the 1988 session pending technical review. As reported the bill includes the changes required by technical review which has been performed.

4:22–25. Repealed by L.1985, c. 433, § 3, eff. Jan. 13, 1986

C. PENALTIES; RECOVERY

4:22–26. Acts constituting cruelty in general; penalty

A person who shall:

a. Overdrive, overload, drive when overloaded, overwork, torture, torment, deprive of necessary sustenance, or cruelly beat or otherwise abuse or needlessly mutilate or kill a living animal or creature;

b. Cause or procure to be done by his agent, servant, employee or otherwise an act enumerated in subsection "a." of this section;

c. Inflict unnecessary cruelty upon a living animal or creature of which he has charge or custody either as owner or otherwise, or unnecessarily fail to provide it with proper food, drink, shelter or protection from the weather;

d. Receive or offer for sale a horse which by reason of disability, disease or lameness, or any other cause, could not be worked without violating the provisions of this article;

e. Keep, use, be connected with or interested in the management of, or receive money or other consideration for the admission of a person to, a place kept or used for the purpose of fighting or baiting a living animal or creature;

f. Be present and witness, pay admission to, encourage, aid or assist in an activity enumerated in subsection "e." of this section;

g. Permit or suffer a place owned or controlled by him to be used as provided in subsection "e." of this section;

h. Carry, or cause to be carried, a living animal or creature in or upon a vehicle or otherwise, in a cruel or inhuman manner;

i. Use a dog or dogs for the purpose of drawing or helping to draw a vehicle for business purposes;

j. Impound or confine or cause to be impounded or confined in a pound or other place a living animal or creature, and shall fail to supply it during such confinement with a sufficient quantity of good and wholesome food and water;

k. Abandon a maimed, sick, infirm or disabled animal or creature to die in a public place;

l. Willfully sell, or offer to sell, use, expose, or cause or permit to be sold or offered for sale, used or exposed, a horse or other animal having the disease known as glanders or farcy, or other contagious or infectious disease dangerous to the health or life of human beings or animals, or who shall, when any such disease is beyond recovery, refuse, upon demand, to deprive the animal of life;

m. Own, operate, manage or conduct a roadside stand or market for the sale of merchandise along a public street or highway; or a shopping mall, or a part of the premises thereof; and keep a living animal or creature confined, or allowed to roam in an area whether or not the area is enclosed, on these premises as an exhibit; except that this subsection shall not be applicable to: a pet shop licensed pursuant to

P.L.1941, c. 151 (C. 4:19–15.1 et seq.); a person who keeps an animal, in a humane manner, for the purpose of the protection of the premises; or a recognized breeders' association, a 4–H club, an educational agricultural program, an equestrian team, a humane society or other similar charitable or nonprofit organization conducting an exhibition, show or performance;

n. Keep or exhibit a wild animal at a roadside stand or market located along a public street or highway of this State; a gasoline station; or a shopping mall, or a part of the premises thereof;

o. Sell, offer for sale, barter or give away or display live baby chicks, ducklings or other fowl or rabbits, turtles or chameleons which have been dyed or artificially colored or otherwise treated so as to impart to them an artificial color;

p. Use any animal, reptile, or fowl for the purpose of soliciting any alms, collections, contributions, subscriptions, donations, or payment of money except in connection with exhibitions, shows or performances conducted in a bona fide manner by recognized breeders' associations, 4–H clubs or other similar bona fide organizations;

q. Sell or offer for sale, barter, or give away living rabbits, turtles, baby chicks, ducklings or other fowl under 2 two months of age, for use as household or domestic pets;

r. Sell, offer for sale, barter or give away living baby chicks, ducklings or other fowl, or rabbits, turtles or chameleons under 2 two months of age for any purpose not prohibited by subsection q. of this section and who shall fail to provide proper facilities for the care of such animals;

s. Artificially mark sheep or cattle, or cause them to be marked, by cropping or cutting off both ears, cropping or cutting either ear more than 1 one inch from the tip end thereof, or half cropping or cutting both ears or either ear more than 1 one inch from the tip end thereof, or who shall have or keep in his possession sheep or cattle, which he claims to own, marked contrary to this subsection unless they were bought in market or of a stranger;

t. Abandon a dog or cat domesticated animal;

u. For amusement or gain, cause, allow, or permit the fighting or baiting of a living animal or creature;

v. Own, possess, keep, train, promote, purchase, or knowingly sell a living animal or creature for the purpose of fighting or baiting that animal or creature; or

w. Gamble on the outcome of a fight involving a living animal or creature—

Shall forfeit and pay a sum not to exceed $250.00, except in the case of a violation of subsection "t." a mandatory sum of $500, and $1,000 if the violation occurs on or near a roadway, to be sued for and recovered, with costs, in a civil action by any person in the name of the New Jersey Society for the Prevention of Cruelty to Animals.

Amended by L.1974, c. 18, § 1, eff. April 11, 1974; L.1977, c. 229, § 2, eff. Sept. 20, 1977; L.1983, c. 103, § 1, eff. March 14, 1983; L.1989, c. 35, § 2, eff. March 7, 1989; L.1991, c. 108, § 2, eff. April 19, 1991.

Assembly Conservation and Natural Resources Committee Statement
Senate, No. 230—L.1991, c. 108

The Assembly Conservation and Natural Resources Committee favorably reports Senate Bill No. 230 1R with Assembly committee amendments.

This bill would increase the penalties for abandoning an animal.

Currently, it is a disorderly persons offense to abandon an animal. This bill would require that the maximum $1,000 criminal fine associated with a disorderly persons offense be mandatorily imposed in the case of abandoning a domesticated animal. The bill would also expand the civil offense of abandoning a dog or cat to apply to the abandonment of any domesticated animal, and increase the amount that may be recovered in a civil action brought by the New Jersey Society for the Prevention of Cruelty to Animals for a violation thereof from an amount not to exceed $250 to a mandatory $500, and $1,000 if the violation occurs on or near a roadway.

The committee amended the bill to update it in keeping with current law and to make it identical with Assembly Bill No. 3562, which was also released by the committee.

4:22–28. Effect of indictment or holding person to bail on liability for penalty

The indictment of a person under the provisions of this article, or the holding of a person to bail to await the action of a grand jury or ~~County Court~~ court, shall not in any way relieve him from his liability to be sued for the penalty in paragraphs "e," "f," ~~and~~ "g," "u," "v," or "w" of section 4:22–26 of this Title.

Amended by L.1989, c. 35, § 3, eff. March 7, 1989.

4:22–29. Jurisdiction of action for penalty

The action for the penalty prescribed in ~~section~~ R.S.4:22–26 or R.S.4:22–27 [1] ~~of this Title~~, shall be brought:

a. In ~~a County~~ the Superior Court, ~~county district court, or a criminal judicial district court, of the county where the defendant resides or in which the offense was committed~~; or

b. In a municipal court of the municipality wherein the defendant resides or where the offense was committed.

Amended by L.1991, c. 91, § 176, eff. April 9, 1991.

[1] Section 4:22–27 repealed by L.1954, c. 50, § 2.

D. ARREST, SEARCHES, SEIZURES, ETC.

4:22–47. Entry, arrests and seizures in building where violations of § 4:22–24 exist

A sheriff, undersheriff, constable, police officer or agent of the New Jersey Society for the Prevention of Cruelty to Animals, may enter any building or place where there is an exhibition of the fighting or baiting of a living animal or creature, ~~or~~ where preparations are being made for such an exhibition, or where a violation otherwise of R.S. 4:22–24 is occurring, arrest without warrant all persons there present, and take possession of all living animals or creatures engaged in fighting or there found and all implements or appliances used or to be used in such exhibition.

Amended by L.1989, c. 35, § 4, eff. March 7, 1989.

4:22–48. Forfeiture of creatures and articles seized under § 4:22–47; costs payable by owner

The person seizing animals, creatures, implements or appliances as authorized in section 4:22–47 of this Title, shall, within 24 hours thereafter, apply to a court of competent jurisdiction to have the same forfeited and sold.

If, upon the hearing of the application, it is found and adjudged that at the time of the seizure the animals, creatures, implements or appliances were engaged or used in violation of section 4:22–47 or paragraphs "e," "f," ~~and~~ "g," "u," "v," or "w" of section 4:22–26 of this Title, or were owned, possessed or kept with the intent that they should be so engaged or used, they shall be adjudged forfeited, and the court shall order the same sold in such manner as it shall deem proper, and after deducting the costs and expenses, shall dispose of the proceeds as provided in section 4:22–55 of this Title.

A bird or animal found or adjudged to be of no use or value may be liberated or disposed of as directed by the court.

The costs of sheltering, caring for, treating, and if necessary, destroying an animal or creature, including veterinary expenses therefor, until the animal or creature is adjudged forfeited and sold, liberated, or disposed of pursuant to this section shall be borne by the owner of the animal or creature.

A creature or property which is adjudged not forfeited shall be returned to the owner, and the person making the seizure shall pay all costs and expenses thereof.

Amended by L.1989, c. 35, § 5, eff. March 7, 1989.

4:22–48.1. Authorization for shelter, care, and treatment of seized animal; destruction; payment of costs; immunity from liability

a. A person authorized to take possession of a living animal or creature pursuant to R.S. 4:22–47 may provide such shelter, care, and treatment therefor, including veterinary care and treatment, that is reasonably necessary, the costs of which shall be borne by the owner of the seized animal or creature.

b. Notwithstanding the provisions of R.S. 4:22–48 to the contrary, a person seizing a living animal or creature pursuant to R.S. 4:22–47 may destroy it before it is adjudged forfeited if the animal or creature is thought to be beyond reasonable hope of recovery, the cost of which destruction shall be borne by the owner of the seized animal or creature. A person destroying an animal or creature pursuant to the authority of this subsection shall not be liable therefor to the owner of the animal or creature.

L.1989, c. 35, § 6, eff. March 7, 1989.

4:22–50.1. Arrest of owner or operator of animal pound or shelter for cruelty; petition to remove and appoint receiver; service

When the owner or operator of an animal pound or shelter is arrested pursuant to the provisions of article 2 of chapter 22 of Title 4 of the Revised Statutes [1] by an agent of the New Jersey Society for the Prevention of Cruelty to Animals or any other person authorized to make the arrest under that article, or when the warrant is issued for the arrest, the person making the arrest or any other officer or agent of the New Jersey Society for the Prevention of Cruelty to Animals may petition the Chancery Division of Superior Court to remove the owner or operator as custodian of the animals and appoint a receiver to operate the pound or shelter. The petitioner shall serve a copy of the petition on the Department of Health, the local board of health, and the owner or operator.

L.1986, c. 89, § 1, eff. Aug. 14, 1986.

[1] Sections 4:22–15 to 4:22–55.

Assembly Economic Development and Agriculture Committee Statement

Assembly, No. 412—L. 1986, c. 89

This bill authorizes and specifies the conditions under which receivers may be appointed for animal pounds and shelters by the courts. Presently, if an owner or operator of a pound or shelter is arrested for cruelty to animals, there are no provisions for the interim care of these animals. As a result, the animals are often left in the care of the person already suspected of cruelty. The bill protects the animals by permitting a court to appoint a receiver to operate the animal facility following the arrest. The court is required, however, to hold a hearing giving the operator the opportunity to contest the initial imposition of the receivership unless the court finds that immediate and irreparable harm may occur to the animals.

Once the receivership is imposed, the court may, upon a finding that the conditions that led to the original charge have been abated, terminate the receivership, subject to any conditions it deems necessary to prevent a recurrence.

The committee amended the bill to modify procedures regarding the receiverships as follows:

1. The petition to put the animal shelter under receivership may be filed only by the person making the arrest or by officers and agents of the New Jersey Society for the Prevention of Cruelty to Animals other than the one who made the arrest. Previously, the bill also permitted members of the society other than the one who made the arrest to file the petition.

2. The petitioner is required to serve a copy of the petition to the owner or operator in addition to serving it to the Department of Health and the local board of health as previously required.

3. The receiver is held liable for any costs of the receivership which result from the gross negligence, incompetence, or intentional misconduct of the receiver.

The other amendments are technical in nature.

4:22–50.2. Appointment of receiver

The court may appoint a responsible person as a receiver upon a finding that the appointment is in the best interests of the animals at the pound or shelter.

A court shall not appoint a receiver without a hearing except upon a finding that immediate and irreparable harm to the animals may result. The owner shall be given notice of the hearing in a manner designated by the court. After receipt of this notice the owner shall be granted an opportunity to contest the imposition of the receivership at the hearing.

L.1986, c. 89, § 2, eff. Aug. 14, 1986.

4:22–50.3. Receiver; authority and duties; compensation; excess revenues; cost deficiency; bond

The receiver shall be the custodian of the animals at the pound or shelter and shall have control over all real and personal property necessary for the daily operation of the pound or shelter. The receiver may assume the role of the administrator of the pound or shelter and take control of the daily operations or direct the owner or operator in the performance of his duties.

The court shall allow from the revenues of the pound or shelter a reasonable amount of compensation for the expenditures and services of the receiver. The revenues in excess of the cost of the receivership are to be paid to the owner of the pound or shelter. The owner is liable for a deficiency in the costs of the receivership, unless the deficiency results from the gross negligence, incompetence, or intentional misconduct of the receiver, in which case the receiver shall be liable for the deficiency. The receiver may be required to furnish a bond, the amount and form of which shall be approved by the court. The cost of the bond shall be paid for by the shelter or pound.

L.1986, c. 89, § 3, eff. Aug. 14, 1986.

4:22–50.4. Reports of actions taken and accounts itemizing revenues and expenditures; presentation or settlement of accounts

The court shall require the filing, at periodic intervals, of reports of action taken by the receiver and of accounts itemizing the revenues and expenditures. The reports shall be open to inspection to all parties to the case. Upon motion of the court, the receiver, or owner or operator, the court may require a presentation or settlement of the accounts. Notice of a motion for presentation or settlement of the accounts shall be served on the owner or operator or any party of record who appeared in the proceeding and any party in interest in the revenues and expenditures.

L.1986, c. 89, § 4, eff. Aug. 14, 1986.

4:22–50.5. Termination of receivership

The receiver, owner, or operator may make a motion to terminate the receivership on grounds that the conditions complained of have been eliminated or remedied. The court may immediately terminate the receivership, or terminate the receivership subject to the terms the court deems necessary or appropriate to prevent the condition complained of from recurring.

L.1986, c. 89, § 5, eff. Aug. 14, 1986.

4:22–50.6. Application of act

This act applies to pounds and shelters as defined and licensed pursuant to P.L.1941, c. 151 (C.4:19–15.1 et seq.); to pounds and places of confinement owned and operated by municipalities, counties, or regional governmental authorities; and to every contractual warden or impounding service.

L.1986, c. 89, § 6, eff. Aug. 14, 1986.

14

British Dangerous Dog Act

THIRTY-THREE days after its introduction, Britain's Dangerous Dog Act was passed on July 25, 1991.

The implementation of the act was divided into three phases. As of August 12, 1991, the four breeds named in the act were required to be muzzled and leashed when appearing in public. By midnight October 12, 1991, these dogs had to be registered with the police. The final phase would occur on November 30, 1991, when all banned dogs must have their exemption certificates, for possession of one of these dogs on December 1, 1991, would be a criminal offense without such a certificate.

The hasty passage of the act took everyone by surprise and left a large number of issues unresolved. Notification and implementation of the provisions of the act were a disaster. The mere expenses of exemption, including registration, neutering, microchip implantation for identification purposes, tattooing, secure enclosures and third-party insurance requirements, left many owners with no other choice than to have their dogs destroyed. Furthermore, many vets were not equipped for tattooing, police departments either didn't

Sr. Antonio Nores Martinez, the developer of the Argentine Dogo.

A champion in the breed's homeland and on the rolls of the Argentine Dogo Club of America is Ch. Alto Chocori Del Choyo, imported and owned by Deidre E. Gannon and Linda Smith. Chocori is a multiple Best in Show winner in Argentina and at rare breed shows in the United States. *Rick Tomita*

have or ran out of required forms and insurance was almost impossible to obtain.

The net effect of the act was to make criminals out of previously honest, law-abiding citizens. Everyone, owners and dogs alike, became guilty until proven innocent.

The "pit bull" type of dogs suffered the most, as they were present in relatively large numbers. The one Tosa Ken present has been targeted since he first arrived and his owners have complied as completely as possible in a poorly run system, including neutering the dog.

Of the four breeds banned in Britain, a multitude of information has been provided on the "Pit Bull" and the Tosa Ken, both of which have at some point in their histories been used as fighting dogs. However, little has been published on the two non-fighting breeds—the Dogo Argentino and the Fila Brasileiro.

While both the Dogo and the Fila hail from South America and are well established in the United States, to the best of our knowledge there are no specimens of either breed in Great Britain. How, then, can a breed that does not exist in a country be banned?

It has been said that two relatively obscure South American breeds were included in the ban in order to comply with the European law requirement that four breeds must be listed in order for the ban to be imposed. However, relying on obscurity as a reason is shortsighted for a ban that had, and still has, the potential to be adopted by many other countries. Australia, Denmark, Ireland and Norway have already followed suit.

It is interesting to note that Dogo breeders in the United States have been contacted by people from Great Britain asking to visit their kennels to see what the uproar is all about.

While not everyone will have the opportunity to have a personal experience with one of the banned breeds, the least owners and breeders have the right to expect is that those with the power to affect their dogs have some basic information as to their origins, purpose and temperament before

Oona De Agallas, owned by Roslyn Apt and Kenneth Johnson, a Dogo bitch with natural ears.

A Dogo puppy, "Hunter," poses with his Boxer chum "Logan." Both dogs are owned by Brian and Janine Westenberger.

making any irrevocable decisions. What follows is the result of many years of research, discussion and direct experience with two of these breeds. You be the judge.

Argentine Dogo

The origin of the Argentine Dogo, or Dogo Argentino as he is known internationally, is as intriguing as the breed itself.

The events that would lead to the need for a large game hunter uniquely suited to the Argentine countryside began innocuously enough in 1908. At that time a number of European wild boars were imported for a local hunting preserve. For years these pigs were safely contained within acres of fenced land. As wild boars produce only one get per breeding, their numbers increased slowly.

The problems began when the owner of the preserve ran into financial difficulties. As fencing was a scarce commodity, it was also expensive, so he began selling off portions of the fencing enclosing the preserve. With the barriers removed, the boar population began roaming the surrounding countryside. Breedings with domestic pigs resulted in offspring that were capable of producing two to four get per breeding, causing their numbers to increase dramatically. Eventually, a migration pattern across Argentina developed, with the ensuing predation problems these animals represented.

In order to reduce numbers and remedy the predatory threat, a form of hunting known as the *montería criolla* was organized. Dr. Carlos Mari, a hunter and Dogo fancier, describes the *montería* as "consisting of the location, chase, reach, capture and killing of the large game predators of our agricultural livestock in their natural habitat, utilizing as a weapon only the hunter's astuteness, trained dogs and a knife."

In Europe, the *montería* was a sport of nobles using packs of fifty or more dogs. However, Argentina presented a completely different environment. The varied terrain and accompanying vegetation precluded the use of large packs of dogs. Thus the search for a breed suited to the Argentine hunting environment began. While some existing breeds possessed one or more of the desired characteristics, not one had them all. Since there was no known breed in the country or one available for importation, the need for a new breed of dog became apparent.

So at sixteen years of age, Antonio Nores Martínez was already conceptualizing his ideal hunting dog. As he studied the attributes dictated by the terrain and the intended prey, his mental pictures solidified and were later reduced to detailed drawings.

Antonio, with the able assistance of his younger brother Augustín, began the act of creation in 1926. While it would take many years to perfect, this young man would ultimately present an invaluable gift not only to his native land but to the world. Augustín, an attorney and diplomat, would then become instrumental in promoting the breed throughout the world and achieving international recognition. Today, the two youngest Nores Martínez brothers, José Luis and Francisco, continue the legacy their brothers created.

As intended and carefully developed, this Great White Boar Hunter is a masterful blend of the best qualities possessed by ten distinct breeds.

As a starting point, the Dog of Córdoba, now extinct, was selected because of his courage, tenacity and strength. Himself a mixture of Mastiff, Bull Terrier, Bulldog and Boxer, he had the requisite head and jaw structure that was of primary importance in a large game hunter. However, he lacked speed and scenting ability. Thus, the Irish Wolfhound was used to provide swiftness and the Pointer added his scenting prowess. The other seven breeds were selected to further develop or enhance traits already present: Great Dane to increase size and improve the head; Great Pyrenees to accentuate the white coat and adaptability to all climates; Bulldog and Bull Terrier to maintain courage, endurance and tenacity; Dogue de Bordeaux to improve jaw strength; Spanish Mastiff for increased strength and power; and finally the Boxer for his keen intelligence and outgoing personality.

The final product was, and is, a dog sound in mind and body with an extremely stable temperament.

The Dogo is a complete package, from his almost infallible nose to his powerful, balancing tail. He participates in the hunt from start to finish, unlike many breeds that have more specialized functions. Structurally, think of him as a finely developed Olympic athlete. While large and well muscled, he is also extremely agile and possesses legendary courage. The Dogo profile exhibits clear, clean lines with a white coat that appears almost painted on his body. The ears are functionally cropped short, which is probably the biggest factor leading to the mistaken classification of the breed as a "big white pit bull."

However, it is the stability of temperament and the multi-functional working abilities of the Dogo that have attracted large numbers of serious fanciers to this unspoiled breed.

Personality-wise, the Dogo reminds me of the Boxer. He is people-friendly and loves to kiss. The biggest problem most exhibitors have is keeping all four of a Dogo's feet on the ground and the tongue off the judge's face. However, his friendly attitude should not lead anyone to underestimate the intelligence and abilities of this breed.

The Dogo has a lot of self-confidence and need not demonstrate his capabilities unless absolutely necessary. He is a natural protector that will react in the face of a direct threat to himself or his family. However, as he possesses an intimidating appearance and a deep, loud bark, most potential intruders/muggers will think twice about taking on a Dogo. Once the Dogo learns what is normal in the neighborhood, he will react only to the abnormal, which makes him a relatively quiet companion animal in the home. However, when a Dogo goes off he should be taken seriously, because something is definitely wrong. Most Dogo owners trust their dog's judgment implicitly.

Though the natural protectiveness will come out only when

absolutely necessary, the native intelligence of this thinking breed is always apparent. These dogs require firm and consistent handling, for when given an inch they will gladly take a mile. They can also be quite inventive if left to their own devices.

All of these factors coming together in one breed have enabled the Dogo to excel at many different tasks. To date there has not been an activity that the Dogo has proven incapable of performing.

His natural scenting ability has been put to use in drug detection and search-and-rescue work. His intelligence, climatic adaptability and strength have been utilized by Independence Dogs in training service Dogos for the mobility-impaired. His athletic abilities make the agility course seem easy to everyone but his handler. His trainability and multi-functional characteristics have seen limited use in Schutz-hund and French Ring Sport. Many also earned Canine Good Citizen (CGC), Temperament Testing (TT) and Therapy Dogs International (TDI) certifications as well as obedience titles.

Fila Brasileiro

The Fila is the national dog of Brazil. While there is still some debate as to his exact origin, artistic works and skeletal remains have established his existence around 481–500 A.D.

The Fila has historically been a working dog, used primarily in outlying areas, on farms and sugar plantations where he served as a cattle driver, guardian and, until the end of slavery in 1886, to search out and hold runaway slaves. Today he primarily functions as a guard dog. His fierce loyalty to his family spawned the Brazilian proverb "Faithful as a Fila."

The Fila is probably one of the most misunderstood breeds in existence today. The problems lie in both descriptive lan-

Fila Brasileiro Club of America Ch. Amigo De Cachoeria Do Fandango, TT was the top winning Fila in the United States for 1989, 1990, and 1991. This imposing animal is owned by Pearl De Ridder. *Bruce Harkins*

Fila Brasileiro Club of America Ch. Aries Sadie of Tazmania, TT, owned by Frank De Ridder, was the top Fila bitch in the United States in 1991.
Bruce Harkins

Five-week-old Fila puppies bred by Frank and Pearl De Ridder.

162

guage and breed perception combined with a failure to differentiate between temperament and behavior.

Temperament is an inherited trait. The Fila temperament is one of intense loyalty and devotion to his family combined with a stable, self-confident demeanor. Behavior, on the other hand, is the response of the dog to an outside stimulus. The Fila is exceedingly protective of all that is his. However, a Fila will rarely display aggressiveness toward another dog. In addition, a Fila that possesses the proper temperament will not be seen to lunge at people for no reason. Rather the Fila will remain between the handler and the other person in case a threat presents itself.

Probably the biggest barrier to appreciating the Fila for what he is, and should be, is the proliferation of mixed-breed dogs possessing Fila pedigrees (e.g., Fila–Neapolitan Mastiff crosses). Thus, there is an organization in Brazil that registers dogs as purebred Filas by inspection only and requires rigorous records to preserve the breed. A similar group has formed in the United States, having been authorized by the Brazilian organization.

15

Selecting and Communicating
With Your Attorney

I F YOU are fortunate enough to find and retain an attorney who also happens to be a dog person, you should have little problem communicating effectively with him or her. This chapter, however, is for the majority who must retain legal counsel who hasn't the vaguest idea what you are talking about.

While it is true that legal dog problems are usually basic legal problems, it is often difficult for the attorney to plow through the surrounding dog matters to get to the real dispute. In addition, dog disputes are emotionally charged and it is difficult to reassure a client when you don't understand all the contributing factors in the situation. For the same reason that many attorneys will not handle matters of family law, many will not take on dog cases, at least not after the first one.

In trying to find legal counsel, first ask other dog people whom they have used. If this search does not produce a name, then contact your local kennel club and ask if any of the members are attorneys or if they can recommend someone. Next consult the legal referral services in your community to see what they would recommend. They may also be able to narrow your situation down and assist you in seeking attorneys in specific areas of practice. Then consult the "general practice" section in the phone book. Sometimes there will be someone with an animal or agricultural law listing. If you have narrowed the situation down to a specific area (e.g. contract, real estate, etc.), check those areas of practice. If not, stay with those listing general practices. Another possibility, if you have not been able to narrow the problem down to a specific area, is to call a known dog/animal law attorney and ask him to direct you to a specific area. While he will not be able to represent you, he can at least help you narrow the search and even assist with the presentation method at the initial consultation.

When you call for an appointment, state the legal category first, but make sure you mention that dogs are involved (e.g., "I have a contract dispute involving dogs and I would like to make an appointment to see Ms. So-and-So"). If that attorney has decided at some point that she doesn't want to handle dog cases, it will keep you from wasting your time and hers. If you are given an appointment, then you will have notified her that you are dealing with a contract dispute. Dogs, at the moment, are secondary.

Before your appointment, prepare a chronological summary of the events leading up to the dispute. Focus on the pertinent facts as much as possible. No matter how upset you are by the situation, remain calm and review the events dispassionately. Once you have narrowed the events down, review them for what dog-oriented information the attorney may need to understand. Think about how you would explain this to a complete stranger who has never owned or shown a dog in his life. Keep it very basic and don't ramble.

During the consultation, expect to be asked questions that will expand on the information you gave initially. You may also be asked about other documentation and what you are seeking to accomplish in pursuing this matter. At the end of the interview the attorney will tell you one of several options: what she intends to do and what she expects it will accomplish; offer to look into the matter further or decline representation. She will also explain any retainer she may require and estimate the fees and expenses you should expect to incur at certain points during the process.

As stated previously, financial considerations are important in dog matters, as any damages you may recover are likely to be minimal. Lawyers and litigation are expensive. If the fees and expenses are beyond what you want to spend or can afford, ask about alternative methods of resolving the dispute. Pennsylvania has a group of retired judges who will mediate a dispute. New Jersey has mandatory mediation for cases in Small Claims and Special Civil Part. There are professional arbitration associations that may be willing to deal with the matter, but, here again, the expenses may be high. Neighbor disputes can also be handled by local hearing panels. Be sure to check if an attorney will be allowed to represent you during these procedures. In some there can be actual representation while in others the attorney may be present to advise you privately but cannot actually participate in the process. Also, make sure that these are not binding so that you can proceed further if you are not satisfied with the decision or recommended settlement.

Regardless of which path you take, start from the very beginning to document everything. Keep a chronological list of everything that happens. Take pictures if they would be helpful to the case. While your attorney will determine what proof is required, it is better for you to have too much rather than too little. Immediate documentation is the best guideline to follow.

Follow your attorney's advice to the letter. When you attend a dog show, don't discuss the matter with everyone on the showgrounds if he has advised you not to say anything. If he hasn't said anything about discussing the matter, ask specifically whether you should. However, you should tell him what a showgrounds can be like. Remember, you never know who knows somebody else who may overhear your conversation. The best general rule is to keep your business to yourself.

In Conclusion . . .

Despite the title, this book is far from complete.

The law in this area will continue to evolve on both the national and international fronts. Many issues have yet to be raised and resolved. However, it is hoped that there will be a trend towards greater uniformity.

Our role, as dog owners, is to develop an acute sensitivity to emerging issues in the community, the state and the nation. Merely reacting to a given situation when it arises is no longer effective. Instead, we must become active participants in shaping our own future.

Remember the adage: If you fool me once, shame on you; if you fool me twice, shame on me.

Statewide Federations, Coalitions, Associations

The American Kennel Club's Special number for legislative matters is 800-AKC-TELL

Arizona Dog Council
Mildred Gleeson, Treasurer
10642 N. 68th Place
Scottsdale, AZ 85254
(602) 948-6904

Responsible Dog Owners of the
  Golden State
Bill Hemby, President
Kevin Belcastro, Director
2400 Darwin Street
Sacramento, CA 95825-0106
(916) 321-3742

California Federation of Dog Clubs
Paullet De Long, Secretary
19500 Clement Drive
Castro Valley, CA 94552
Susan Hamil, Legislation
(714) 494-9506

Colorado Dog Fanciers Association
Mickey Rubin, Legislation
1856 S. Columbine
Denver, CO 80210
(303) 722-0161

Connecticut Dog Federation, Inc.
Diane Taylor, President
43 Umpawaug Rd.
W. Redding, CT 06896
(203) 938-3152

Florida Association of Kennel Clubs
Diane Albers, President
401 Cardinal Oaks Court
Lake Mary, FL 32746
(407) 322-8980 Home

Georgia Coalition of Dog Clubs
Cindy Goodman, President
3939 Pate Road
Loganville, GA 30249
(404) 985-6769

Illinois Dog Clubs and Breeders
  Association
Sandra Bamberger, Chair
532 65th Street
Clarendon Hills, IL 60514
(708) 971-2364

Kansas Kennel Club Association
Ramona Adams, President
32783 215th Street
Easton, KS 66020
(913) 773-8558

Responsible Dog Owners of LA
Donald Kirsch, Secretary/Treasurer
P.O. Box #9196
Metairie, LA 70055-9196
(504) 837-7038

Federation of Maine Dog Clubs
Nola Soper, Newsletter
P.O. Box 577
Bucksport, ME 04416
(207) 469-3852

Dog Owners' Guild of Maryland
Barbara Davis, Legislative Chair
2121 Belfast Road
Sparks, MD 21152-9760
(410) 472-3479

Massachusetts Federation of Dog
  Clubs & Responsible Dog Owners
Virginia Rowland, President
P.O. Box 325
Templeton, MA 01468-0325
(508) 939-5300

Michigan Association for Pure-
  Bred Dogs
Richard McClure, President
122 South Street
Belleville, MI 48111
(313) 697-1181

Michigan Federation of Dog Clubs
Stephanie Katz, President
1701 Strathcona Drive
Detroit, MI 48203
(313) 368-3123

Minnesota Council of Dog Clubs
Sherry Bakko, Secretary
596 Ottawa Avenue
St. Paul, MN 55107
(612) 227-2639

Missouri Federation of Animal
  Owners
Karen Strange, President
P.O. Box 554
Eldon, MO 65026
(314) 392-4850

Dog Owners of the Granite State
Jan Mullen-Stewart, President
165 Dover Point Road
Dover, NH 03820
(603) 742-0205

New Jersey Federation of Dog Clubs
Diane Rau, President
P.O. Box 4348
Warren, NJ 07059-0348
(908) 469-1754

New Mexico Federation of Dog
  Owners
Pat Bouldin
P.O. Box 91894
Albuquerque, NM 87199
(505) 345-4889

Associated Dog Clubs of New York
  State
Gordon Carvill, President
RD 1, Miller Rd.
East Greenbush, NY 12061
(518) 477-5266
(518) 477-9555

Responsible Dog Owners
  Association of New York
Ann Lettis
91 Wiman Avenue
Staten Island, NY 10308
(718) 317-5804

Confederacy of Tailwaggers
Steve Wallis, Legislative Chair
6000 High Bluff Court
Raleigh, NC 27612
(919) 782-2558

Responsible Dog Owners of Ohio
Dr. Alan Riga
6325 Aldenham Drive
Mayfield Heights, OH 44143
(216) 449-3662

Oklahoma Dog Fanciers Coalition
Donna Danner, Legislative Director
P.O. Box 27691
Tulsa, OK 74149
(918) 587-3811

OK K-9 Legislative Alliance
Wendy Musgrove, Chair
700 NW 22nd Street
Oklahoma City, OK 73103
(405) 528-5181 Home
(405) 524-7587 Work

Responsible Dog Breeders
  Association of Oregon
Patti Strand, President
4141 SE 141st Avenue
Portland, OR 97236
(503) 761-8962

Pennsylvania Federation of Dog
  Clubs
Dotsie Keith, Legislative Chair
P.O. Box 67
Furlong, PA 18925
(215) 794-7173
Information Phone
(215) 842-2407

South Carolina Federation of Dog
  Clubs
Don Wilson, President
Peggy Wilson, Secretary
908 Cedar Springs Road
Blythewood, SC 29016
(803) 754-4880

Responsible Animal Owners of
  Tennessee
Donna Malone, President
3327 Lockmeade
Memphis, TN 38127
(901) 353-1805

Tennessee Dog Federation
MaryAnne Armbruster Smith,
  Secretary
536 Paragon Mills Rd.
Nashville, TN 37211

Associated Dog Clubs of Texas
Steve Schmidt, President
1713 Ross
Carrollton, TX 75006
(214) 242-1078
(214) 358-3362

Responsible Pet Owners Alliance
  (TX)
Mary Beth Duerler, President
14350 Marin Hollow
Helotes, TX 78023
(210) 695-3388

Texas Coalition of Responsible
  Animal Owners
Robert Rohr, President
P.O. Box 294914
Lewisville, TX 75029-4914

Utah Dog Fanciers Association
Evelyn Bohac, Secretary/Treasurer
384 East 200th North
Lindon, UT 84042
(801) 785-1750

Vermont Federation of Dog Clubs
Ann Thornhill, Secretary
RD 1, Box 80
North Ferrisburg, VT 05473

VA Federation of Dog Clubs &
  Breeders
June Zink, Legislative Committee
6031 Woodpecker Road
Chesterfield, VA 23832
(804) 590-1811

West Virginia Federation Dog Clubs
Gene Conley, President
Route 1, Box 209
Mt. Clare, WV 26408-9718
(304) 622-3014

Dog Federation of Wisconsin
Don Heibler, President
4231 North 87th Street
Milwaukee, WI 53222
(414) 463-2614

Regional Federations, Coalitions, Associations

Responsible Dog Breeders of San Mateo County
Dr. James Boso, President
400 Walnut Street, Suite 350
Redwood City, CA 94063
(415) 851-4403

Responsible Pet Owners of Northern California
Julie Kelley
5101 Maynard Road
Palo Cedro, CA 96073
(916) 547-4741

Sacramento Council of Dog Clubs
Joan Gibson Reid
P.O. Box 215126
Sacramento, CA 95821-9998
(916) 689-1661

Paws Across Florida
Marge Mowl
P.O. Box 171
Largo, FL 34649-0171
(813) 584-6991

Protecting Our Pets
Chris Walkowicz
RR 1 Box CA 33
Sherrard, IL 61281-9801

Montgomery County Animal Fanciers
Ruth Berman
P.O. Box 59660
Potomac, MD 20859

Paws Across New Jersey
Marianne Lawrence
P.O. Box 317
Howell, NJ 07731
(908) 928-0087

Long Island Coalition of Dog Fanciers
Sue Weiss
25 Lotus Street
Cedarhurst, NY 11516
(516) 569-2168

Associated Dog Clubs of Austin
Sue Slaughter
7906 Creekmere Lane
Austin, TX 78748
(512) 282-3423